Urban appropriation and transformation: bicycle taxi and handcart operators in Mzuzu, Malawi

Ignasio Malizani Jimu

Langaa Research & Publishing CIG
Mankon, Bamenda

Publisher:
Langaa RPCIG
(*Langaa* Research & Publishing Common Initiative Group)
P.O. Box 902 Mankon
Bamenda
North West Province
Cameroon
Langaagrp@gmail.com
www.langaapublisher.com

Distributed outside N. America by African Books Collective
orders@africanbookscollective.com
www.africanbookscollective.com

Distributed in N. America by Michigan State University Press
msupress@msu.edu
www.msupress.msu.edu

ISBN:9956-558-75-3

First published 2008

DISCLAIMER

All views expressed in this publication are those of the author and do not necessarily reflect the views of Langaa RPCIG.

Francis B. Nyamnjoh
Stories from Abakwa
Mind Searching
The Disillusioned African
The Convert
Souls Forgotten
Married But Available

Dibussi Tande
No Turning Back. Poems of Freedom 1990-1993

Kangsen Feka Wakai
Fragmented Melodies

Ntemfac Ofege
Namondo. Child of the Water Spirits
Hot Water for the Famous Seven

Emmanuel Fru Doh
Not Yet Damascus
The Fire Within
Africa's Political Wastelands: The Bastardization
of Cameroon

Thomas Jing
Tale of an African Woman

Peter Wuteh Vakunta
Grassfields Stories from Cameroon
Green Rape: Poetry for the Environment
Majunga Tok: Poems in Pidgin English
Cry, My Beloved Africa

Ba'bila Mutia
Coils of Mortal Flesh

Kehbuma Langmia
Titabet and the Takumbeng

Victor Elame Musinga
The Barn
The Tragedy of Mr. No Balance

Ngessimo Mathe Mutaka
Building Capacity: Using TEFL and African
Languages as Development-oriented Literacy
Tools

Milton Krieger
Cameroon's Social Democratic Front: Its History
and Prospects as an Opposition Political Party,
1990-2011

Sammy Oke Akombi
The Raped Amulet
The Woman Who Ate Python & Other Stories
Beware the Drives: Book of Verse

Susan Nkwentie Nde
Precipice

**Francis B. Nyamnjoh &
Richard Fonteh Akum**
The Cameroon GCE Crisis: A Test of
Anglophone Solidarity

Joyce Ashuntantang & Dibussi Tande
Their Champagne Party Will End! Poems in
Honor of Bate Besong

Emmanuel Achu
Disturbing the Peace

Rosemary Ekosso
The House of Falling Women

Peterkins Manyong
God the Politician

George Ngwane
The Power in the Writer: Collected Essays on
Culture, Democracy & Development in Africa

John Percival
The 1961 Cameroon Plebiscite: Choice or Betrayal

Albert Azeyeh
Réussite scolaire, faillite sociale : généalogie
mentale de la crise de l'Afrique noire francophone

Aloysius Ajab Amin & Jean-Luc Dubois
Croissance et développement au Cameroun :
d'une croissance équilibrée à un développement
équitable

Carlson Anyangwe
Imperialistic Politics in Cameroun:
Resistance & the Inception of the Restoration of
the Statehood of Southern Cameroons

Excel Tse Chinepoh & Ntemfac A.N. Ofege
The Adventures of Chimangwe

Bill F. Ndi
K'Cracy, Trees in the Storm and Other Poems

**Kathryn Toure, Therese Mungah
Shalo Tchombe & Thierry Karsenti**
ICT and Changing Mindsets in Education

Charles Alobwed'Epie
The Day God Blinked

G.D. Nyamndi
Babi Yar Symphony

Samuel Ebelle Kingue
Si Dieu était tout un Chacun de chacun?

Ignasio Malizani Jimu
Urban Appropriation and Transformation:
bicycle, taxi and handcart operators in Mzuzu,
Malawi

To

Mahala and Luntha

Contents

List of Figures

List of Tables

List of Photos

Acronyms

EIU Economist Intelligence Unit

GDP Gross Domestic Product

ILO International Labour Organisation

IMF International Monetary Fund

JCE Junior Certificate of Education

MBOA Mzuzu Bicycle Operators Association

MSCE Malawi School Certificate of Education

MUFIS Malawi Union for Informal Sector

MWK Malawi Kwacha (currency of Malawi)

NSO National Statistical Office

PSLCE Primary School Leaving Certificate of Education

SAPs Structural Adjustment Policies

THA Traditional Housing Area

UNCHS United Nations Centre for Human Settlements - HABITAT

WEAZ Workers Education Association of Zambia

WOW War on Want

Acknowledgements

I wish to thank the bicycle taxi and handcart operators who participated in this study. Thanks too to Fariot Ngwira and Hendrix Kayuni who, when students of Chancellor College at the University of Malawi, assisted with data collection between January and March 2006. Thanks also go to my colleagues and friends in the Department of Geography. Special thanks to Golden Msilimba, Kenneth Tchuwa, Gift Dube and Mphatso Kadaluka (Physical Planning Department in Mzuzu). Kenneth Tchuwa introduced me to a rich source of social statistics in Malawi and drew the map of Mzuzu city.

In a special way, I wish to thank Professor Francis B. Nyamnjoh. It is through his inspiration and encouragement that I considered releasing results of this study in the form of a book.

Thanks too to my wife Nellie, our two children, and my parents.

Summary

This book presents the lives of bicycle taxi and handcart operators in Mzuzu city in Malawi. My interest in these people emerged while I was studying informal economy organisations in Blantyre and Mzuzu as part of a comparative project covering five African countries: Ghana, Malawi, Mozambique, South Africa and Zambia (War on Want et al., 2006). I thus set out to investigate the dynamics of the sub-sector of the informal economy comprising bicycle taxi and handcart operators, with particular attention to the socio-economic characteristics of the operators.

Findings of the investigation reveal that handcarts have been a versatile and long established means of transport in Mzuzu, while bicycle taxis had been on the scene for just over three and a half years. Both modes of transport are the most visible and mobile feature of the informal economy of Mzuzu city after the relocation of street vendors in mid-2006. A casual visitor to the city cannot fail to notice the contribution that the workers in the sub-sector make to the mobility and economic life of many people.

Bicycle taxi and handcart activities are similar to other informal activities in that there are few barriers to entry and operations typically rely on diverse sources of funding. These activities stand out as creative and imaginative ways of appropriating urbanisation. Bicycle taxi and handcart or wheelbarrow operators facilitate mobility of both people and goods in the formal and informal economies, with the impact felt mainly by informal economy workers, most of whom reside in low income and high density unplanned housing estates. By linking various economic activities and urban spaces, bicycle taxis and handcarts serve as modes of urban transformation.

While attempting to understand the dynamics of informal transport opportunities, the study also tried to document the perceptions of informal economy workers of the world around them and their perceptions of the role they play in the social and economic (re)construction of urban societies. It was difficult to get substantive information on daily incomes as well as quantifiable linkages with other sectors of the economy of Mzuzu city, which confirms observations in other studies on the unavailability of data on several aspects of the informal economy. However, qualitative assessments and other indirect measures reveal that these activities are significant and the level of significance is obvious in social and employment indicators: proxy indices of income earned, spent and hence redistributed; existence or absence of alternative livelihood activities; uses of incomes; linkages with other economic and social activities; and advantages cited by operators and their clients on the operational efficiency of the two modes of transport.

This study, like ones previous to it, illuminates linkages between rapid urbanisation and growth of the informal economy, intensity of rural-urban migration and changing dynamics in the informal economy. For instance, the study shows that most of the people involved in bicycle taxi and handcart operations are recent rural-urban migrants. Most of the operators come from surrounding districts, mainly from Mzimba. The major reason driving people into the informal sector is economic desperation. Therefore, these activities are in every sense marginal or refugee occupations. Considering the sources of and capital requirements, the informal economy develops usually without state subsidized credit. However, the informal economy workers are always eager to receive support from the state in the form of loans or through creation of better and more employment opportunities that can absorb unemployed youths, including those working in the informal economy. In the final analysis, this study helps us understand how people straddle formal and informal sectors and multiple challenges and opportunities in order to survive when the state's macro-economics fail.

Chapter One

OVERVIEW OF THE STUDY

Historically, towns and cities have been centres of economic and social development. New ideas and new and exciting jobs and other socio-economic opportunities continue to be linked to urbanisation. Urbanisation involves more than a mere increase in the number of people living and working in towns and cities. It is driven by a series of interrelated processes of economic, demographic, political, cultural, technological and social change. The structure of urbanisation is influenced by past and present decisions about land use, transportation and economic development; political processes and representation; and social planning. Yet, the study of the growth of urban areas is often reduced to the population factor, that is the growth of urban population through natural increase and immigration. Natural increase refers to population growth resulting from more births than deaths in a population. As more people are born than are dying, the population of a town or city grows progressively. Migration is influenced by a number of factors commonly described as push and pull factors. Positive net rural-urban migration, like natural increase, also has the effect of swelling urban populations. In most developing countries, it is the second factor – immigration – that contributes to much of the growth of towns and cities, especially in many sub Saharan African countries, including Malawi.

Malawi is experiencing high rates of rural-urban migration and also high urban growth rates (United Nations, 2004). It is estimated that every year many young people flock from rural areas to the towns and cities to look for better socio-economic opportunities associated throughout historical times with cities. The economic challenges that recent rural-urban migrants encounter, at least in the initial stages of their stay in towns and cities, revolve around limited employment opportunities and slim chances of ever getting meaningful and rewarding employment. By implication, many recent rural-urban migrants accept any work that comes their way. Those with low education attainment are more vulnerable to unemployment (Jimu, 2003) and as has been observed in many cities of the developing world, most of them end up in the informal economy (Fapohunda, 1985; Hart, 1973; Hope 1996). Informality though difficult to define is characterized by unconventional actions taken by individuals with the aim of meeting needs.

According to Laguerre (1994:32) informality is characterized by the intention or personal needs of the actor, with the individual often aware of his or her unconventional action. No wonder that informality constitutes activities that are not officially recognized by the formal societal system (Laguerre, 1994:30). Informality applies to a whole range of needs and activities, be they sourcing, producing or distributing food, clothing or shelter. Informality is a norm in most developing countries, especially in those where the liberalisation of the economies in the 1980s to 1990s led to de-industrialisation (Harrigan, 2001).

The study of urban informality reveals the important role of the informal economy in the process of urbanisation. In the case of Malawi, it is now acknowledged that rapid urbanisation leads to informality even in the provision of housing and shelter as manifested by the proliferation of squatter settlements, which are associated with temporary structure, congestion and sanitation breakdowns (Phiri, 2004). Urban poverty, pegged at over 60 percent at the end of the 20th century, is on the rise. In situations where the poor outnumber the better off, poverty becomes acceptable as a norm, to the extent that the poor become invisible not by their physical absence but through under representation of their interests and trivialisation of the various informal ways or activities upon which their survival is structured. As minorities who are in the majority, informal workers cease to exist in the sense that they are least heard. Activities that make them economic citizens of the cities and towns are trivialized by the authorities. Trivialisation of informality is common in Malawi in general and Mzuzu city in particular. Informality is regarded as a problem. Informality is incompatible with the values of a significant number of people, who are more organized or in positions of leadership as well as more powerful in economic, social and political affairs (Outhwaite and Bottomore, 1993), which in essence leaves out the views of silent majorities. This means that informality becomes a problem once it is designated as harmful, and calls are made for improvement. The challenge of such designation is illustrated by the case of bicycle taxis and handcart or wheelbarrow operators in Mzuzu.

Bicycle taxi and more so handcart or wheelbarrow operators have been plying their trade for several years now and for as long as half a generation in the case of some handcart operators, yet there is little recognition of the role they play in the economy of which they are a part, neither research outputs nor policies initiatives towards encouraging or promoting these creative enterprises. Newspaper reports, however, do recognize these economic operators, but in a way that questions the very existence of non-motorized modes of transport in the cities and with a tone that is degrading to the humanity of the operators and disparaging to the users of such services. The operators and their clients are characterized as objects of urban poverty and underdevelopment, rather than as active agents involved in the construction of landscapes of activity. Little is said or implied that acknowledges that behind the operators are real people who are also heads of families and their families and kin with needs just like anyone else. It less appreciated that such lines of kinship cut across the rural-urban divide since multi-locality of members of the same households is common and often seen as a strategy of improving the socio-economic situation of household members. No wonder some scholars consider the distinction between "urban" and "rural" poverty as artificial given the strong linkages between rural and urban areas (Satterthwaite, 2000). It is these aspects of the socio-economic reality of the bicycle taxi and handcart or wheelbarrow operators in Mzuzu city that are core to this study.

Nature of the study

This book is about the experiences of urbanisation by a group of young men involved in a nascent or emerging informal economy sub-sector of informal non-motorized transport in the form of bicycle taxi and handcart or wheelbarrow operators. The terms handcart and wheelbarrow are used interchangeably as explained in chapter six. I have known and interacted countless times with the bicycle taxi and handcart or wheelbarrow operators for the past few years. As a geographer with a noticeable bias toward development studies, especially rural-urban linkages, unemployment and poverty as they are experienced by those working in the informal economy, I became curious seeing handcart or wheelbarrow operators right on my first visit to Malawi's northern city of Mzuzu and the first hint of bicycle taxi operations when the practice was just emerging. Bicycle taxi and handcart operators represent in my view a new wave of urbanism. Urbanism is used in this context to refer to forms of social interaction and ways of life that develop in urban settings (Knox, 1994). Bicycle taxis and handcarts represent transport options with significant socio-economic and environmental benefits. Relatively lower costs make them convenient options for passenger and freight services for the low income and over relatively longer distances.

Through internet searches, I discovered that bicycle taxis in particular are also popular in East Africa. The popularity of bicycle taxis is revealed by the numerous local names used in different countries and places. For example, in the eastern Ugandan towns of Busia and Jinja, bicycle taxis are known as *boda boda* (BBC, 2001), while in Burundi they are known as push peddlers. In Southeast Asia, non-motorized taxis are called rickshaws. In Mzuzu bicycle taxis are known affectionately as *Sacramentos*, a name derived from Sacramento speed buses, introduced after Shire Bus Lines, a state-run company with buses known for frequent breakdowns, was on the verge of dissolution. The new and robust Sacramento buses usually operated between Blantyre in the South and Karonga in the North.

While official discourse on pro-poor growth is dominated by the need to empower the poor economically, there is little in the way of giving the poorest of poor the means to come out of poverty. Instead, those who try to exercise ingenuity by creatively savaging disparate situations, created by the failure of the state to provide essential goods and services and employment, are quite often the subject of state sponsored stigma and oppression. An example is the repression of street vending without providing sufficient alternative operating sites. The case studies of bicycle taxi and handcart operators show that although economic conditions are precarious or uncertain, informal economy workers are not simply people who have lost out on the struggle for formal economy opportunities. Rather they are people attempting and in meaningful ways to address the real causes of poverty at a level that even the state with its agents of development and oppression cannot reach.

Framework of the study

Modernisation theory maintains that urbanisation is part of the natural transition from a traditional society to a modern nation, while urban bias theorists argue that government policies biased in favour of urban areas encourage migration from the countryside to towns and cities (Lipton, 1977). According to Michael Lipton, urban bias is manifested by rural projects that are less well designed than urban ones, poor prices for agricultural produce, poor funding for agricultural projects and poor infrastructural development. There are few incentives for doctors, bankers, and engineers to go to rural areas, yet common are measures enticing private rural savings to flow to industrial investment. The value of industrial output is artificially high, and emphasis on industrial development pushes resources away from activities that could benefit the poor in rural areas. Rural area development plans that give priority to agriculture get lip service but the city gets the resources. As if all this were not enough, there is also lack of power to organize the pressure that could challenge the power of elites and turn rhetoric into distributive action. From these two standpoints, rapid urbanisation can be seen as a positive process that should be encouraged or one that leads to temporary urban economic growth but in the long term brings a plethora of social and economic problems.

Contemporary studies of urbanisation in the developing world have focused on the growth of urban populations, the evolution of diverse livelihood activities, most of which are informal, and economic experiences that ensue (Fapohunda, 1985; Hart, 1973; Jimu, 2003; Post 1996). Diversity of livelihood strategies has been portrayed in development literature as part and parcel of the de-agrarianisation trends, that is, a process of reorientation from rural agricultural to urban and non-agricultural economies (Bryceson, 1996). Ellis and Freeman (2002) have shown that the encompassing character of the livelihoods concept means that almost any aspect of the way people go about gaining a living is potentially legitimate to investigate. Although this is rarely appreciated, the purpose of investigating livelihood strategies should however be to understand the factors that shape various livelihood activities in order to shed light on how and when individuals, households, and groups negotiate among themselves and with their communities, markets and society to improve their well being or reduce insecurity by appropriating the benefits from their assets, activities, and investments (Valdivia and Quiroz, 2001). Rural-urban linkages such as rural-urban migration, remittances sent by urban migrants, and flows of goods to and fro, just to mention a few, are part of household livelihood diversification strategy (Tacoli, 1998). Hence it is pertinent to understand the impact of seasonal labour migration of people back and forth between city and countryside, and the significance of remittances from rural migrants working in urban areas to their families from one locale to the other. Interestingly a consensus is emerging that these are the major means by which rural-urban migrants negotiate informally the administrative and metaphorical boundaries that separate the rural from urban. It is then argued that one of the core questions should be how to accommodate or create space in policy and physical planning for the ever growing population(s) involved in diversified urban livelihood portfolios collectively known as the informal economy (Hope, 1996, 2001; Jimu, 2003; Post, 1996).

Apparently ever since the publication of Keith Hart's article (1973) on 'Informal income opportunities and urban employment in Ghana,' the informal economy has become recognized as one of the manifestations and in other situations a characteristic feature of recent and rootless rural-urban migrants, most of whom have residence in informal settlements that are also characterized by high levels of urban poverty. Hart argued that the urban poor were not 'unemployed,' rather they were working, although often for low and erratic returns. In a recent write up, Hart emphasised that 'informal' incomes, unregulated by law and invisible to bureaucracy, are a significant part of urban economies that have grown up largely without official knowledge or control (Hart, 2007).

On the origins of urban poverty, Ilife (1987) noted that in colonial times most of the poor in African towns were unskilled labourers. Ilife further noted that urban settlers were poor when they were unemployed; when they worked in especially ill-paid occupations; when they had unusually large families; or when general wages were especially low. Africans migrating to Malawi's only major town of Blantyre in colonial times created collections of badly built, unsanitary and densely packed huts of a temporary character all around the margins of the town, and the colonial government was too poor to provide a better alternative (Ilife, 1987). In recent times, rural-urban migration is not a problem in itself, rather the intolerable push conditions in the villages as well as the appearances of success –real or imagined – pushing or pulling either way the disenchanted or enthusiastic villagers and over time leading to swelling armies of urban poor and unemployed people. The fact that levels of poverty and diminishing opportunities in rural areas are in most circumstances higher than in urban areas strengthens premises of the urban bias thesis. Peterson (1965:7) echoed this observation some forty years ago when he remarked that:

> Only a small minority of the migrants need realize their expectations in order for the myth to survive that opportunities in the cities are greater.

Dasgupta (1973) observed in the case of Bengali immigrants to Calcutta that they usually came to the city in years of bad harvest with the hope that the government would be more likely to take heed of their plight than if they stayed in remote villages. Although most of them returned to their rural homes when conditions improved, some made the cities and slums of Calcutta their home and swelled the ranks of the city's informal sector.

Data and methods

The study was based on both primary and secondary data. In order to accomplish the task, I employed a complex sampling technique and a variety of data collection strategies. It will be appreciated that the study was largely qualitative in nature. The total sample size for the survey was 40. Twenty-one of the participants were bicycle taxi operators and the other nineteen were wheelbarrow operators. The participants were chosen at random using the snowball and cluster random sampling techniques. Sampling took into account the spatial distribution of the subjects around the city and the fact that the operators happen to be very mobile. This attribute created challenges with respect to identification of the actual participants and the data collection process.

I employed three data collection techniques. Field inspections were carried out in the initial days of the survey to map out fields of activity, in other words the spatial concentration or spread of the bicycle taxi and handcart or wheelbarrow operators and other informal economy activities. I noted the existence of numerous ranks from which the operators plied their trade to various destinations within and outside the city. The ranks were situated at road junctions (such as Namizu, Katoto, Chiputula Junction, and Mwizalero); near big super markets (such as Shoprite and Kandodo); close to produce markets (like Mzuzu Main Market); near hardware shops (H.H. Wholesale rank); and at bus and minibus terminals (Mzuzu Bus Depot).

The second data collection method was the survey whereby interviews were conducted with the chosen 21 bicycle taxi and the 19 handcart operators. A questionnaire comprising both closed and open ended questions was developed. The questionnaire had four sections, on socio-demographic dimensions, economic aspects, characteristics of clients, and the spatial issues. Several other questions or themes were identified for focus group discussions. Two groups, one of bicycle taxi operators and the other made up of handcart operators, were organized. The focus group discussions were designed to generate debate and information sharing among the operators over and above collecting data on the shared values and perceptions of the occupations and challenges that the participants encounter in their work.

I collected life histories of a few bicycle taxi and wheelbarrow operators. The participants described important events and experiences in their lives. The aim was to capture the socio-economic and cultural backgrounds of the individual operators. I found life histories essential as accounts of how the operators came to be bicycle taxi and handcart operators. Although the stories are quite personal and not necessarily representative of the groups, the accounts tell much about the fabric of the bicycle taxi and handcart operators as a social group. The accounts reveal the feelings and perspectives of bicycle taxi and handcart operators regarding the opportunities and challenges of life. It is from the very same accounts that I have been able to make sense of the ways the operators situate themselves in relation to each other and those with whom they interact on a daily basis.

Some respondents were less enthusiastic about responding to questions on their place of residence and the nature of the houses in which they live, hence data collected on some variables did not add up to 40 responses. This was not a serious drawback since the purpose of the study was not to conduct a census. Data collection proceeded quite well. Quantitative data was subjected to computer based analysis using the statistical package for social sciences

(SPSS) version 10.0. Qualitative data was analyzed manually by disaggregating the data according to the core themes, recurrent patterns of thought, perceptions and uniqueness of issues. The core themes are articulated in the final chapter.

Organisation of the book

The book is divided into ten chapters. This chapter is introductory. The context and research questions have been introduced together with the research methodology and research methods. The study can be situated within the ambit of geography and development studies. It draws particularly on the theoretical literature on urbanisation, migration, informal economy, poverty and development. Chapter two provides a succinct overview of literature on the informal economy and the place of the informal economy in development discourses.

Chapters three through five aim at situating the study. Chapter three looks at the geographic position and the demographic and economic situation of Malawi and Mzuzu. It is one the first of its kind to focus on non-motorized transport providers and to introduce Mzuzu city, Malawi's booming third city and centre of administration for the northern region, in the debates on urbanism in Malawi. Chapter four is focused on the process of urbanisation and urban development in Malawi. In this chapter, informality is portrayed as the very fact of rural-urban migration. Urban life bad as it may be portrayed is perceived as an improvement because conditions in cities have always been relatively better than those in rural areas. This is the case even when relatives from the village come to visit their relations with great anticipation but are welcomed by disappointment because of the low standard of living in the city as compared to that in the village (Englund, 2002). Chapter five is an overview of the urban informal economy in Malawi. The chapter emphasizes that despite shifts in economic policy from growth strategy to poverty reduction and recently to growth and development strategy, the underlying causes of poverty are far from being addressed and the only positive development since the mid 1990s appears to be the growth of the informal economy as a grassroots adjustment to glaring and worsening poverty.

Chapter six provides a overview of urban transport in Malawi, the growth of bicycle taxi and handcart modes of transport, and the challenges as well as the solutions from the perspectives of the operators. Chapter seven looks into the social profile of the bicycle taxi and handcart operators. Problems of rapid urbanisation such as deplorable lack of running water; poor sanitation; poor distribution and access to electricity; and unemployment are negotiated through informality. Chapter eight provides an overview of the economic value of the bicycle taxis and handcarts. The ninth chapter explores through qualitative appraisal the reasons leading to the growth in the number of people involved as bicycle taxi and handcart operators.

Drawing mainly on insights from the stories told by the bicycle taxi and handcart operators, the tenth chapter proposes a framework within which to situate the dynamics of bicycle taxi and handcart operators in the informal economy and also suggests strategies for promoting business in the informal economy, with a focus on bicycle taxi and handcart operators. The chapter demonstrates the degree to which the study on bicycle taxi and handcart or wheelbarrow operators in Mzuzu city complements previous studies on urbanisation and rural-urban linkages carried out in other major urban centres in Malawi, especially in Blantyre and Lilongwe.

Chapter Two

OVERVIEW OF THE INFORMAL ECONOMY

The previous chapter has shown that there is a correlation between urbanisation and increasing surplus urban labour on the one hand and the degree of informality in income generating activities on the other. The current chapter underscores this relationship, initially observed and discussed in an in-depth study of the Frafras, one of the northern Ghanaian ethnic groups that migrated to the urban areas of southern Ghana (Hart, 1973). Hart noted that the unskilled and illiterate sub-proletarians pursued a variety of activities that to a great extent changed income and expenditure patterns in a manner that could not be accounted for using economic principles applicable in capitalist economies. Although there is now little disagreement on the importance of the informal economy, there is still a certain degree of discomfort among urban authorities on whether and how to accommodate and nurture it.

This chapter begins with a brief overview of literature on the informal economy. This will situate the discussion of the socio-economic profiles of the bicycle taxi and handcart operators in ongoing debates on the processes of urbanisation and economic decline, and the transformations brought about by economic liberalisation and globalisation. Then, drawing on reformist and 'marginalist' perspectives, the place of the informal economy in the process of development is examined, in particular the contribution of the informal economy towards job creation, income distribution and poverty reduction. The feminist critic of development theory is introduced as an alternative approach to development theory as well as a window for appreciating the gender dynamics of economic life in the informal economy.

Informal economy in perspective

The term informal economy is loosely used to include an enormous diversity of activity that spans the globe and dominates the economy of many developing cities. Brown (2006) noted that the informal economy is difficult to define and even more difficult to measure. Amidst confusion a semblance of consensus seems to be emerging that the informal economy constitutes economic activities, that is the production and distribution of goods and services, which are not registered and regulated by the state or local government in contexts where similar activities are regulated (Bromley, 1998; Jimu, 2003; Sinclair, 1978: 84; United Nations, 1996). As Brown (2006) puts it, the concept informal economy is used to imply economic activities that largely operate outside the national and local legislative or regulatory context. Yet, operating outside the state or local legislative context does not constitute illegal activity.

The intellectual history of the concept dates back to the work of Keith Hart in the early 1970s. Hart (2006) argued that the informal economy was 'provoked by the failure of prevalent economic models to address a large part of the world' for which they claimed to offer prescriptions. Since then, the World Bank and the International Labour Organisation (ILO) have identified the informal economy as something with which they must deal. As Hart (2006) illustrates, whereas once the effects of 'informality' were thought to be palliative, they are now often seen as a threat to 'legitimate' businesses.

In developing countries, the term 'informal sector' has broadly been associated with unregistered and unregulated small-scale activities (enterprises) that generate income and employment for the urban poor (Bernabè, 2002). Terms used to characterize and describe activities carried out in the informal economy include: small-scale or micro-enterprises, subterranean, underground, unofficial, hidden, shadow, invisible, black, second economy (Hope, 2001). These terms describe the informal economy in relation to the formal – the visible, official, large-scale and first or most significant sector comprising government or public service and the private sector. The informal economy can also be defined in terms of its origin by emphasizing the conditions that have made business in the informal economy attractive both to operators and their clients. In this manner, Hope (1997:8) suggested that the informal economy be seen as encompassing activities that have emerged due to the failure of developing countries to formally make the kind of economic progress that would have allowed for, among other benefits, low urban unemployment rates, a reduction in national poverty rates, wages and salaries that keep pace with inflation, the ready availability of basic goods and services, a functioning infrastructure, and a relatively honest and efficient bureaucracy. Taking this as a blueprint, the informal economy defies the limits imposed by formal society with respect to business ethics. However, this characterisation overplays and exaggerates the separateness of the informal economy. In reality formal and informal business entities constitute interlocking economic segments. As elements of the same economy, the trend of late is to think of the two sectors more as attributes of each other and integral to the economic system, hence the use of the term informal economy as opposed to informal sector that was popular until recently (War on Want et al., 2006).

Characteristics of the informal economy

Typical characterisation of the informal economy is that of small scale and labour intensive activities. However, there are different ways of classifying informal economic activities. Brown and Lloyd-Jones classified informal economic activities into four groups; retailing and wholesale; craft, manufacturing and production; services and transport; and construction (Brown and Lloyd-Jones, 2002:189). Bromley (1997) identified nine major categories: retailing, small-scale transport, personal services, security services, gambling services, recuperation, prostitution, begging, and property crimes. Common features about all these categories are low fixed costs, use of simple technology, reliance on family labour, use of personal or informal sources of credit, low or no fixed costs associated with the infrastructure of a shop (rentals, maintenance and security), no payment of taxes, and relatively easy to establish and exit (Fidler and Webster, 1996; Hart, 1973; Hope, 2001). These characteristics sometimes work against the informal economy. According to Bernabè (2002) the informally employed are marginalized and excluded relative to the societies in which they live, which regard informal employment as unworthy and disgraceful. Much qualitative evidence also points to the fact that the informally employed feel powerless to change their lives.

The informally employed are forced into informal employment to survive, because the 'state has abandoned them.' Thus they do not voluntarily exclude themselves, but their exclusion involves an external agent. This characterisation is typified in Table 2.1, which summarize the characteristics of the informal economy in contrast to the formal economy.

Table 2.1 General characteristics of formal and informal economies

Characteristics	Formal economies	Informal economies
Ownership	Corporate ownership	Usually family ownership
Technology	Capital-intensive	Labour intensive
Capital	Relatively abundant	Scarce
Skills	Often acquired within formal education/training	Usually acquired outside formal education systems
Hours of work	Regular system	Irregular
Scale of operations	Large (unless very high-quality product)	Small
Prices	Generally fixed	Usually negotiable (by haggling)
Credit sources	Banks and other formal institutions	Personal, non-institutional sources
Profit margins	Often small per unit but large turnover	Often large per unit but small turnover
Relations with customers	Impersonal and often on paper	Direct and personal
Fixed costs	Substantial	Limited
Publicity	Large-scale and necessary	Usually none except personal recommendations
Re-use of goods	None, gives rise to waste products	Frequent
Government aid	Extensive in many cases	Rare and very limited in quality
Direct dependence on foreign countries	Considerable: essential to many firms	Limited or none

Source: Adapted from Hornby, W.F. and Jones, M. (1991) *An introduction to settlement geography.*

The weakness of this characterisation is that it does not say much about the people involved in the informal economy. In other words, are they any different from those engaged in the formal economy? Coming back to the origins of the informal economy, characterizing the informal economy in terms of people who are actively involved would include survivalists; very poor people doing various income generating activities; self-employed people who produce goods for sale, purchase goods for resale, or offer services; and very small businessmen and women (micro entrepreneurs) (Fidler and Webster, 1996: 6; Jimu, 2003). A more catching characterisation of the informal economy is provided by Hart (2007):

> The label 'informal' may be popular because it is both positive and negative. To act informally is to be free and flexible; but it also refers to what people are not doing – not wearing conventional dress, not being regulated by the state. The 'informal economy' allows academics and bureaucrats to incorporate the teeming street life of exotic cities into their abstract models without having to know what people are really up to.

Talking about the size of the informal economy, conservative estimates in the 1990s showed that the informal economy accounted for up to 40, 55 and 70 percent of total urban and non-agricultural employment in Latin American, Asian and African countries, respectively (Hussmanns, 1996:17). At that moment, in some African countries the informal economy was bigger than the formal economy, comprising well over 70 percent of total gainful employment. For instance, in the 1990s between 80 and 90 percent of the economically active urban population in Tanzania, Burkina Faso and Mali were engaged in the informal economy. In Bamako, the capital of Mali, at least 70 percent of women worked in the informal economy and most households including those with 'salaried workers' were engaged in informal economy activities to supplement income (Colleye, 1996: 153-166). For other countries like Cameroon, Ghana, Nigeria, Togo, Congo and Senegal; the informal economy employed 23.08, 23.2, 30.6, 30.8, 55 and 50 percent of total labour force in the 1990s, respectively (United Nations, 1996). A similar situation prevails in Malawi as illuminated in chapter four.

On the same theme of characteristics of the informal economy, a comparative study on informal economy organisations in Ghana, Malawi, Mozambique and Zambia noted that workers in informal employment can be differentiated from those in the formal economy by examining the lack of arrangements related to seven essential securities (War on Want et al., 2006):

- Labour market security (adequate employment opportunities through high levels of employment ensured by macroeconomic policies);

- Employment security (protection against arbitrary dismissal, regulation on hiring and firing, employment stability compatible with economic dynamism);
- Job security (a niche designated as an occupation or 'career,' the opportunity to develop a sense of occupation through enhancing competences);
- Work security (protection against accidents and illness at work, through safety and health regulations, limits on working time and so on);
- Skill reproduction security (widespread opportunities to gain and retain skills, through innovative means as well as apprenticeships and employment training);
- Income security (provision of adequate incomes); and
- Representation security (protection of collective voice in the labour market through independent trade unions and employers' organisations and social dialogue institutions).

The characteristics presented above do not in any way imply that the informal economy is a completely detached segment; rather the participants have been reduced to a situation of despondency by a failure of the formal economic system to guarantee mass welfare through employment and high levels of income per capita. In this regard, informal economy workers represent a category of workers relegated from the formal 'sector,' though the term formal sector itself is not free of controversy. It is now known that the concept of sectors is misleading since it leads others to think of the sectors as self contained. While not rejecting the formal-informal divide, it is also informative to accept that all sectors in an economy are indeed involved with each other through flows of goods and services (Goldthorpe, 1996) and straddling, a situation whereby people may be active in more than one sector in the course of a day (Niger-Thomas, 2001). The characteristics presented above reveal that the distinction between the formal and informal sector is not just academic but also serves important analytical purposes. This is further underscored theoretically in the subsequent section on the informal economy and development discourses and practically in the struggles that the informal economy workers undergo in the conduct of business in Mzuzu and other urban and rural areas in Malawi, particularly outlined in chapter seven.

The informal economy and the development debate

Bernabè (2002) shows that there have been two main parts to the informal economy debate. The first, which dominated much of the 1970s and 1980s, focused on the informal-formal sector relationship. Those who supported the 'duality approach' argued that there were two distinct urban economies (the poor/informally unemployed vs. the rich/formally employed), while their critics saw these as two aspects of the same, single, capitalist economy. The second, which took off in the late 1980s in Latin America with the publication of de Soto's (1989) work on Peru, is concerned with the causes of the informal sector: is the primary cause of the informal sector poverty or excess regulation? The ideas of these two schools of thought are discussed in the next paragraphs, from a development theory perspective, as either following reformist or neo-Marxist perspectives.

The term 'informal sector' emerged in the 1970s (Bernabè, 2002). This was a period of crisis in development theory since the 'accelerated growth model' postulated in the 1950s and 1960s had not succeeded in creating employment and eliminating poverty in developing countries. Unprecedented population growth, as of the 1950s, coupled with increased rural-urban migration, and an inability of the industrialisation process to absorb the large numbers of unskilled, illiterate workers resulted in widespread poverty and unemployment. It became apparent that the urban poor were not actually 'unemployed' but engaged in a multitude of small-scale, unregistered, unmeasured and largely unregulated activities. Ever since the early 1970s, debates have polarized into two schools of thought, namely the reformist perspective, which in essence is informed by modernisation theory, and the neo-Marxist perspective, informed by the dependency paradigm or school (Nattrass, 1987). The diverging theories are instrumental in understanding the role and function of the informal economy as well as the perceptions of different categories of people towards those engaged in the informal economy.

The reformist school as championed by the International Labour Organisation (ILO) mission to Kenya in the 1970s and the World Bank situates the informal economy as an important sector having vast potential for vitalizing employment creation, job training, entrepreneurial skills development, and economic growth (Fapohunda, 1985; UN, 1996). In this regard the informal economy is not marginal because it can be profitable and efficient. This view has been echoed innumerable times in the literature on the role of the informal sector in developing countries, particularly those undergoing economic reform or crises and experiencing rising levels of unemployment or underemployment and abject poverty. The informal economy is then partly too wholly due to slow economic growth or decline of the formal economy (Hope, 1997, 2001; Rogerson and Hart, 1989). In these contexts, the reformist position is that the competitiveness of the informal economy derives from a lack of bureaucratic and hierarchical structures, and unregulated operating environments that make business cost-effective and more profitable to the participants. There is an understanding that to enhance the benefits emanating from the informal economy focus should be on the promotion of an environment free from bureaucratic constraints (Ajayi, 1996: 162). However, lack of regulation in itself is a disincentive. In situations where regulation is associated with ability and willingness to pay taxes, lack thereof compromises the vitality of the informal economy. As a non tax paying sector, governments are swift to disregard or at best to ignore it completely with grave consequences like: inadequate provisions for premises and space, inadequate access to credit and finance, inadequate social infrastructure and other public support and development assistance, and sometimes outright repression (Esim, 1996: 142-3; Jimu, 2003; United Nations, 1996: 17; Walker, 1996: 130-131). What is needed therefore are steps and policies to enhance the capacity of the informal economy by ameliorating the disadvantages of informality mentioned above.

The neo-Marxist school on the other hand focuses on the structural relations between the formal and informal sectors of an economy. The informal economy is a 'marginal' sector, involving 'petty commodity production.' As a 'marginal' or a 'petty commodity production' sector, neo-Marxists contend that the informal economy is just a distinct 'marginal pole' which, by acting as a reserve army of labour and producing cheap, poor quality, subsistence goods, facilitates capital accumulation in the formal sector (Cross, 1998; Moser 1978; Tokman, 1978). Hernando de Soto (1989) argued that informality is a response to inappropriate regulation and that the informal operators find it almost impossible to comply with bureaucratic requirements for operating businesses (Brown, 2006). In many cases the informal economy is a low productive sector often associated with goods and services that do not conform to any definable standards. By implication, the participants in the informal economy or the 'lumpen proletariat' (Fapohunda, 1985: 19) make little contribution to gross domestic product (GDP). It was on this account that Biplab Dasgupta

(1973: 72) noted some three decades ago on the vitality of Calcutta's informal sector that:

> A second feature of the informal sector in Calcutta is that most of those engaged in it are workers in unskilled or obsolete occupations, which make little contribution to the national economy.

As he further put it there could be very little loss to the economy as a whole if the informal economy workers were removed from their occupations. This was a hostile view of the informal economy that manifests itself in Malawi today in different forms. This perspective underscores the notion that local or national authorities engrossed in this line of thinking can hardly appreciate the vitality of the informal economy or even consider the need to provide space for informal economy operators.

Recent studies have however shown that the informal sector is not just subordinate to the formal sector, but that it compliments the formal economy. I observed some three years ago that street vending in Blantyre and all Malawi's towns and cities is a case in point and indeed complements formal retail outlets (Jimu, 2003). Similarly, Emizet (1998: 129) argued that although both informal and formal sectors of an economy are subordinate to the structural constraints of the broader or total economy, the informal economy is a challenge to the formal sector because it enhances social justice by accommodating marginalized people, by undermining and even displacing the formal economy. From these accounts, 'marginalist' interpretations of the informal economy are disputable and at the present moment not substantiated by facts since in most developing countries the model of state-led development alongside a vibrant big business sector has failed to materialize and to generate an expanding and efficient modern sector. Far from disappearing in the face of economic development, informal activities are on the increase in poor developing countries as well as in many middle-income and high-income industrialized countries. In an environment of formal sector recession and disintegration, the informal economy provides avenues for invigorating economic rejuvenation (Hussmanns, 1996: 15; Meagher, 1995: 261).

Which way forward for the informal economy

Increasing unemployment and/or a burgeoning informal economy may arise where formal firms or the public sector are not expanding quickly relative to labour market supply. Some national contexts could include (Altman, 2007):

- rapid urban migration caused by push/pull factors such as diminished rural livelihood opportunities and large rural-urban wage gaps;
- economic growth and development that leads to rising capital intensity and industrial concentration that reduces the pace of formal employment growth; this is particularly found in resource-based exporting economies;
- public sector downsizing or restructuring;
- an unsuccessful trade liberalisation that reduces formal employment opportunities;
- pro-cyclical fiscal policy that exacerbates the decline in formal activity during a downturn;
- monetary policy that is insufficiently conducive to the sustained growth of new labour absorbing activity, for example where currencies are volatile and/or overvalued as often found in resource-based economies or those affected by portfolio flows.

The view that the informal economy serves the interests of the underprivileged sounds quite good; yet the beneficiaries are not always the poorest of poor. Wherever the informal economy workers have had problems with agents of modernisation like the state and formal business, the modernisation mission has been articulated to the disadvantage of the poor. Is it not worrisome that urban planning is heavily biased in favour of 'modern' business ventures and against the myriad of unregulated activities. Post (1996: 5) articulated this view by noting that although in most developing countries the informal economy administers to the needs of a large urban population, it is often seen as reminiscent of the past and is swept into a pile labelled chaotic, untidy, unhealthy and illegal. As Post further put it, this approach ignores the incapacity of the formal economic sector in cities and towns to absorb everyone seeking employment. Post therefore advocated for 'space' for the informal economy given its capacity to meet the needs of poor people and of those marginally employed and struggling to survive. The survival of the informal economy, bad as it may be portrayed, signifies that it offers opportunities. In the era of globalisation, the advantage is that in most cases businesses in the informal economy are citizen owned, locally controlled and less susceptible to economic hardships as compared to large ones (Briscoe, 1995). This however is unlikely to remain the case because foreigners have already joined the informal business sector, as is the case of Nigerians, Tanzanians and other nationalities in Malawi and Zambians and Zimbabweans in Botswana and South Africa.

There is a gender component to the informal economy in that men have traditionally controlled a disproportionate share of formal positions and women's work is predominantly informal. Studies in Africa and other countries in the developing world, indicate that women constitute the principal labour force in the informal sector, particularly in such activities as food and beverages, retail trade, pottery, basket weaving and cross border trade (Murry, 1991; Niger-Thomas, 2000; United Nations, 1996). A sectoral analysis of women's participation in the informal sector in Congo, Gambia and Zambia indicates that women are highly involved, accounting for 94.1, 88.9 and 90.6 percent of retailers, respectively (United Nations, 1996: 11). Even in South Africa, women constitute the majority of participants in the informal sector (Friedman & Hambridge, 1991). The dominance of female participants in the informal sector is a factor of low education and employable skill levels among women, which preclude a majority of them from directly enjoying the benefits of a growing formal sector. However, radical feminists would argue that the trend reflects the gender imbalances inherent in patriarchal societal arrangements, ones that favour males to females, in education, skill training and employment. Women are relegated to the informal sector. Mitullah (2003) also found a strong gender bias in the informal economy, whereby the majority of street traders tended to be women. Most of the women in the informal economy were workers, sole breadwinners, widows or deserted by spouses. They had limited education though younger women had higher education levels, and many joined the informal economy because of lack of other employment opportunities. These realities have led activist groups- such as Women in Informal Employment: Globalizing and Organizing (WIEGO) and the Self Employed Women's Association (SEWA), to use the concept of gender as an umbrella concept drawing attention to discrimination worldwide (Hart, 2007).

Conclusion

The informal economy is by no means a new economic sector. Nor do informal economy workers constitute a separate sector. Rapid growth of the informal economy in recent times reflects slow economic growth, shortfalls in meaningful employment opportunities and therefore the creativity cum ingenuity of the masses denied or deprived access to orthodox and formal economic opportunities. Individuals and households with inadequate incomes participate in the informal economy to meet minimum daily nutritional requirements, as well as other needs such as clothing, education, and transportation. In these respects, the informal economy is not a diseconomy to the national economy. In fact informal and formal economies complement each other such that it is intricate to disentangle them even using the most sophisticated economic analysis tools. Boundaries between informal and formal economies are difficult if not impossible to establish. In terms of development, it is compelling to argue that each sector makes a remarkable contribution. The informal sector has implications for social policy, labour market development, public finance, law and national accounting.

The informal sector provides a considerable source of income and employment in countries where formal employment opportunities are limited and social security almost non-existent. Informal economy dynamics are further illustrated in the next two chapters in which I present the national context of the study and the extent to which the character of the informal economy reflects national as well as broader regional and global socio-economic and political trends.

Chapter Three

CONTEXT OF THE STUDY

This chapter provides an overview of the national and local context of the study. Economic and social dimensions of the national context are discussed while, for the local context, the geographic position of Mzuzu is presented as well as a historical overview of the development of what is today the third largest urban settlement in Malawi and a regional administrative centre for the North. I have also sketched the development prospects of the city that is slowly becoming the hub of international or cross-border informal trade with Tanzania. The chapter ends with a projection of the future role of Mzuzu city in regional and national development.

Geographic position

Geographically, Malawi is a small country in the heart of southern Africa, lying south of the equator between latitudes 9^0 45′ and 17^0 16′ and between longitudes 33^0 and 36^0 east. In terms of size, Malawi is 840 km long and varies from 80 to 160 km in width. The total area is 118 484 square km of which about 20 percent is water. Prominent physical features are Lake Malawi (also known as Lake Nyasa), which is about 570 km long, ranging from 16 to 80 km in width at 475 meters above sea level, and several mountain ranges and plateaus of which the highest point is Sapitwa on the Mulanje plateau (see Figure 3.1).

Population trends

The distribution of population has not been uniform among the three regions of Malawi. The 1987 census showed that almost half of the population was in the southern region which has about a third of the country's land area. In contrast, the northern region with a quarter of the land area had 11 percent of the population. The population density then was the highest in the South with 125 persons per square kilometre, followed by the Centre and North with 87 and 34 persons per square kilometre respectively. These regional variations are partly a reflection of the disparities in employment opportunities and basic infrastructural facilities.

Figure 3.1 Major settlements in Malawi

Source: Profile for Malawi (Terra Viva! Base Map: Political Boundaries)

The 1999 population estimates showed that the southern region was home to 46 percent of the total population, while the North had 12.5 and the Centre about 41.5 percent. The general trend is that the growth rate as well as actual population living in the South as a percentage of total national population is falling with the passage of time. Between 1987 and 1998, the population living in the North increased from 900 000 to 1.2 million representing a growth of 33.3 percent. During the same time period, the central region registered an increase of 32.2 percent (from 3.1 to 4.1 million) while the South registered a population increase of 15 percent (from 4.0 to 4.6 million). Life expectancy has dropped from 48 years in 1990 to 39 in 1998 and 37.5 in 2002 mostly due to the high incidence of HIV/AIDS, malaria and other killer diseases (AFRODAD, 2005).

Socio-economic context

Malawi has a legacy of 73 years (from 1891 to 1964) of colonial rule. At independence in 1964 from Britain, the economy was rural based, characterized by three main sectors: the estate sector (large foreign-owned farms) producing for export; the smallholder sector (small indigenous-owned farms) producing for subsistence, but also providing marketed food surplus and export crops; and the labour reserve sector supplying estate labour and migrant labour to neighbouring countries (Stambuli, 2002). According to Pryor (1990: 39), at the time of independence many people familiar with the economic situation of Malawi spoke of its lack of economic viability and of the fact that the first president Late Dr Hasting Kamuzu Banda was heading an 'empty government' in a nation with an 'empty economy.' During the first years following independence, Malawi's development strategy focused on open market export oriented growth based on agriculture. Agriculture continues to support 85 percent of the population and accounts for 35 percent of GDP (single largest sector) and 80 percent of the labour force. Agriculture also contributes 90 percent of foreign exchange earnings. The industrial sector is the second most important in terms of output and accounts for about 13 percent of GDP and wage employment (Harrigan, 2001). This sector has, however, been on the decline in the recent past.

During the first thirty years of independence, Malawi was ruled by 'president for life' Dr Hastings Kamuzu Banda whose government pursued policies consciously biased towards supporting the estate sector (Ellis et al., 2003). The ideology was to modernize agriculture, generate economic growth and transform traditional farming practices. This modernisation mission led to the institutionalisation of laws that facilitated land transfer from the smallholder sector to the estate sector and the estate sector had better access to subsidized credit on government guaranteed terms (Stambuli, 2002). The introduction of multi-party politics in 1994 begun the process of redressing some of imbalances, but the processes involved are inevitably slow, uneven, and complicated (Ellis et al., 2003). Smallholder agriculture has not grown as fast as expected because of, among other factors, shortage of arable land against a relatively high population density and lack of access to farm inputs. the situation worsened in the 1990s following the liberalisation of the agricultural sector in the 1980s and the subsequent removal of agricultural subsidies (Ellis et al., 2003; Stambuli, 2003). Initiatives to make fertilizer available in the 1990s, the starter pack and targeted input programmes had short term ameliorative outcomes. The fertilizer subsidy programme introduced in the 2005-06 growing season has, coupled with good climatic conditions, led to food security at national level. The question has always been whether the government has capacity to continue the project. Besides, what are the impacts on livelihoods security since livelihoods are broader than the capacity to produce food.

Other indices of socio-economic well being show that over 70 percent of the population earns no income whatsoever indicating a higher dependency ratio. Seventy percent of the population is unable to read and write, 85 percent lives in rural areas, and women head 34 percent of all households. Only 21 percent of women have continued their education beyond primary school. Recently, high levels of gender based violence and homicide have been partly linked to socio-economic uncertainties. Poverty, which simply means deprivation of basic necessities of life (Chambers, 1989: 1), and the poor – those who even in normal circumstances are unable to feed and clothe themselves properly (MacPhereson & Silburn, 1998: 1) – are a real challenge in both rural and urban areas. Experts on development in Malawi have identified the following key causes of poverty: dependence on agriculture (covered later in the chapter) and lack of other exploitable natural resources, low productivity, depressed world prices for main exports, land lockedness, poor macroeconomic management, and very high rates of HIV/AIDS infection, just to mention a few (Dorward et al., 2003).

Structure of the agricultural sector

From independence to the late 1980s, Malawi's agricultural policy perpetuated colonial neglect and underdevelopment of the smallholder sector (Stambuli, 2002). Throughout this period, great emphasis was on commercial farming of the tradable crops like tobacco, tea and sugar. The government guaranteed bank loans to support estate tobacco farming and put in place other measures to encourage the production of tobacco. Cabinet ministers and other senior civil servants were encouraged to engage in estate tobacco farming. The then head of state, who owned several tobacco estates in different parts of the country, led by example. Press Agriculture, a semi-state organisation, was established and had estates in all three regions of the country that grew tobacco as their main crop. Land use patterns were also altered to accommodate the strategy, prioritising freehold and leasehold capitalist farming units. The Land Acquisition Act of 1965 was enacted to facilitate the transfer of smallholder lands to the estate sector. Leasehold landholdings rose from 79 000 hectares in 1970 to 758 400 hectares by 1989. The number of estates increased from 229 to over 14 000 over the same period. Estate land rose further to 1 000 000 hectares by 1997, well over 10 percent of the total land. The estates had access to collateralized finance secured by the same land acquired from smallholders. This resulted in unprecedented growth in the per capita gross domestic product. These advances were made at the expense of the subsistence-farming sector. There was a favourable tax regime with a land tax of only 10 Kwacha per hectare, which was later raised to 30 Kwacha per hectare. Low land rent means lower opportunity costs of idle land. Stambuli (2002) notes that with lower rents most estate owners kept their land idle. The situation in Kasungu in the central part of the country was that most farmers used about 45 percent only of their land. The government enacted what is known as the Tobacco Act which defined tobacco as a commercial crop that could be grown on leasehold and freehold land only. This meant exclusion of the majority of the smallholder farmers who cultivate on customary land. The impact on development is that it deprived the smallholder farmers of the opportunity to participate in the cultivation of this profitable crop. Tobacco had been a profitable crop from the 1960s until the 1990s. Dr Banda believed that the growth of estate agriculture would create employment for the majority of the people. The labourers on estates would then acquire knowledge and technologies and apply them on their farms. The agricultural labourers were supposedly expected to grow their own food and depend on the wages on estates to support other needs.

The National Salaries and Wages Act of 1968 was designed to keep wages as low as possible in the urban areas thereby discouraging rural-urban migration. Indirectly the policy was meant to make labour available for agricultural development. The maximum Wage Policy was implemented in 1971. This policy required employers seeking to increase wages in excess of 5 percent to apply for approval from the Wages and Salaries Restraint Committee (Torres, 2000). Estates producing tobacco enjoyed lucrative access to international markets through the auction floors.

Policies targeting the smallholder sector were few and dismal in terms of impact on livelihood improvement. Farm inputs especially fertilizer, hybrid seeds and pesticides were subsidized to ensure that they were easily accessible to smallholder farmers. Input subsidies were administered through the Smallholder Farmers Fertilizer Revolving Fund of Malawi (SFFRFM). These farm inputs were however abused in that they were also easily accessed by commercial farmers either through buying off from smallholder farmers or directly procuring from the Agricultural Development and Marketing Corporation (ADMARC) outlets. Excluded from producing tobacco, smallholder farmers concentrated on producing food crops like maize, groundnuts, sorghum, cassava and millet. Smallholder farmers could sell their products to ADMARC only. ADMARC offered very low prices that were barely less than 50 percent of the border prices. ADMARC realized high profits by selling agricultural products acquired at very low prices. Urban bias was manifested by ADMARC's role in subsidizing maize prices for urban consumers and its engagement in unproductive sectors of the economy (Stambuli, 2002). Recent efforts to deregulate the agricultural markets seem to have failed to trigger the expected supply responses. Qualitative assessments of the impact of policy reforms suggest that they have had negative outcomes on the livelihood situation of rural and urban populations dependent on agriculture. The situation is precarious for food crops. Per capita food production and availability declined significantly in the 1990s to early 2000s. Though the reintroduction of the fertilizer subsidy in 2005 has led to some significant improvements in food production, there are numerous structural and institutional constraints to attainment of food security and improved income levels for agricultural producers.

Poverty reduction appears largely unattainable. According to Wobst et al. (2004), some of the key issues are: low level of market development hence excessively low economic activity, lack of economic diversification and the associated risks of poor communication, low development of transport infrastructure hence high transaction costs, limited access to inputs, risks of natural shocks-adverse weather, crop and animal diseases, and physical insecurity as a result of rising crime and political violence. These harsh realities have accelerated urbanisation in the sense that they lead to influxes of people from rural areas to urban centres (United Nations, 2004). Due to urbanisation, poverty is increasing in urban households with homeless migrants living in slums not fit for human habitation (Phiri, 2004). Droughts, prolonged dry spells, and floods have undermined optimism and raised doubts about the sustainability of agro-based livelihoods. Because over 85 percent of the population lives in rural areas, to reduce hunger, poverty and famine there is need to invest in agricultural activities to increase food production and induce economic and rural development. Food production must be integrated into the broader development strategy that includes: empowering women by increasing access to credit, land and education; facilitating the creation of smallholder farm cooperatives and promoting their trading capacity; improving access to local, regional and international markets; as well as harnessing the emerging energy of civil society around agricultural and developmental issues. There is also the need for a proactive approach towards combating the HIV/AIDS crisis that threatens agricultural and economic productivity. Government and development partners must consider these issues seriously and account for them when designing and implementing programs.

Location of Mzuzu

The city of Mzuzu is located in the northern part of Malawi (Figure 3.1) about 370 km to the north of Lilongwe and 47 km to the west of Nkhata Bay, a resort town located on the shores of Lake Malawi. In terms of site, Mzuzu lies on the northern Viphya plateau at an altitude of about 1 600 m (4 200 feet) above sea level. Much of the development is residential in nature. Major residential areas are Chasefu, Chibanja, Chimaliro, Kaning'nina, Katawa, Katoto, Luwinga, Mchengautuwa, Nkhorongo, and Zolozolo (Figure 3.2).

Figure 3.2 Map of Mzuzu city

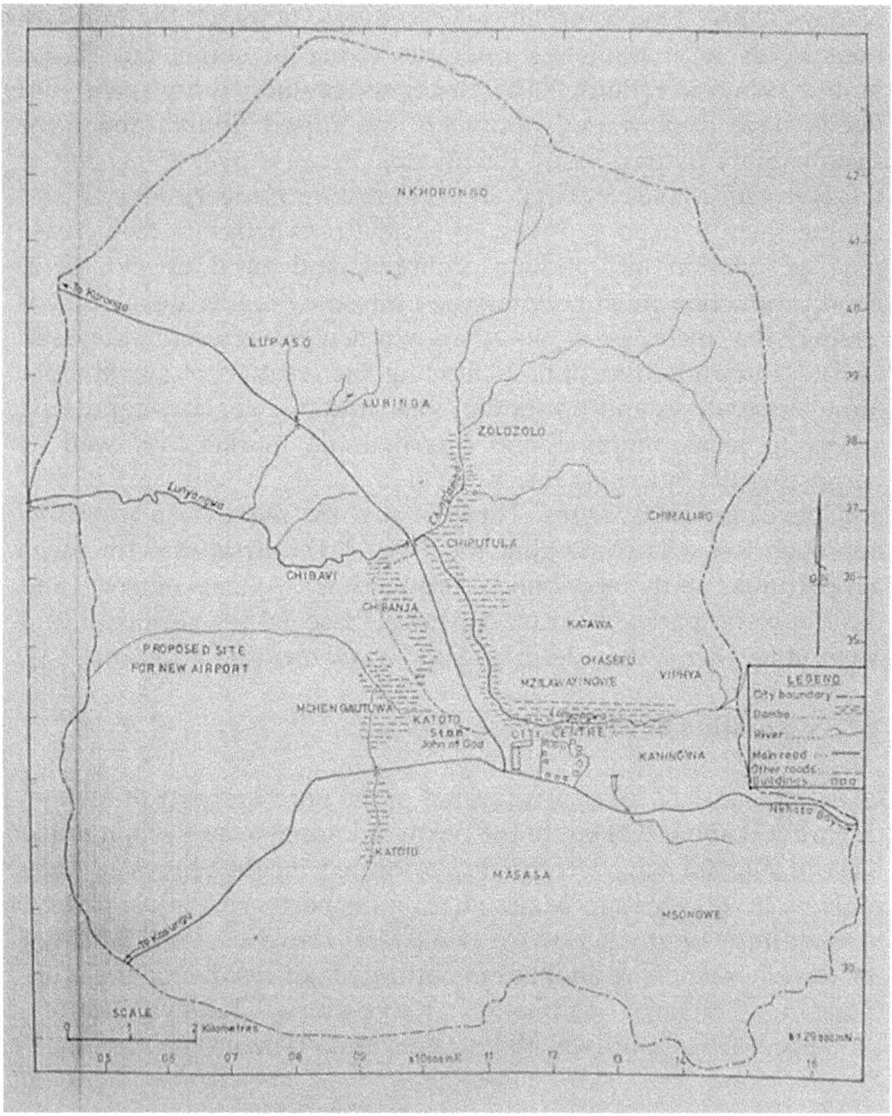

NKHORONGO

To Koronga

LUPASO

LUBINGA

ZOLOZOLO

Luwyanwa

CHIMALIRO

CHIPUTULA

CHIBAVI

CHIRANJA

KATAWA

PROPOSED SITE
FOR NEW AIRPORT

CHASEFU

MZILAWAYINOYE

VIPHYA

MCHENGAUTUWA

KATOTO
Star
John of God

CITY CENTRE

KANINGINA

To Rumphi

Nkhoto Bay

KATOTO

MASASA

MSONGWE

SCALE

2 Kilometres

05   06   07   08   09   x10000mE   11   12   13   14

Historical roots of Mzuzu

Historically, Mzuzu is a recent developer compared to the other three major urban centres of Blantyre, Lilongwe and Zomba. Its history as an urban centre goes back to the last 60 years. Legend has it that the city is named after Msusu stream which is one of the streams crossed by the Mzuzu-Nkhata Bay road. However, the name Msusu changed to Mzuzu when it was discovered that there is another 'Msusu Stream' in Kasungu (Blantyre Newspapers Limited, 1985b). In an undated book titled *People of Mzuzu*, Elva Edson Singini recalls that the name Mzuzu is a corrupted version of a local name for a banana-like plant known as Vizuzu, which was found along a stream near the house of the first European in Mzuzu by the name of Mr Boardman. Both versions on the origin of the name Mzuzu could be correct since it is possible that Vizuzu could be a name referring to trees that grew along Msusu Stream and/or Msusu Stream derived its name from the name of trees that were then predominant or uniquely associated with it. In Malawi many places have names of famous persons and outstanding physical features such as mountains, trees, and rivers. For instance, the capital of Malawi is named after the Lilongwe River while the former capital was named after Zomba mountain or plateau.

Initially, Mzuzu city developed as a Tung settlement soon after the end of the Second World War. This is supported by archival information which suggests that in 1946 a few white settlers opened up the virgin forest land for Tung plantations (for growing trees that produce Tung nuts and oil). However, Mzuzu was officially founded in 1949 by the Colonial Development Corporation (CDC). Some four years later in 1953 Mzuzu was made Provincial Headquarters for the Northern Province even before it was recognized as a town. It was only on January 1, 1966 that Mzuzu was elevated to the status of a township.

Mzuzu became a Municipality on May 1, 1980. Three reasons were given for elevating Mzuzu to the municipality status (Blantyre Newspapers Limited, 1985b). The primary reason was in recognition of the improvement of social services offered to the public. The second reason was rapid population growth. Finally, impressive infrastructural development took place in the town since it became a township 14 years earlier. The print media reported that at the time Mzuzu had basic infrastructure such as health, education and entertainment. Specifically, it had a standard hospital, a government dispensary, a pharmacy, a departmental store, a hotel, three banks, a sports stadium, a teacher training college (TTC), two secondary schools, a technical college, and a private clubhouse. With these developments it did not come as a surprise when five years after becoming a municipality Mzuzu was bestowed the status of a city on September 1, 1985. A spokesman of the then Ministry of Local Government in Lilongwe announced the elevation of Mzuzu to city status by the head of state Dr H. Kamuzu Banda. It was then reported in the local press that elevation of Mzuzu was in recognition of the significance of Mzuzu as the regional and main centre of government administration, commerce and industry in the northern region (Blantyre Newspapers Limited, 1985a). Following the elevation of Mzuzu to city status, a number of public companies opened branches in Mzuzu. Some of them are now in private hands or have closed down due to competition unleashed by economic liberalisation and globalisation and underperformance. The list included Grain and Milling, Press Bakeries, David Whitehead and Sons, New Building Society (NBS Bank), Press Shire Clothing and Old Mutual (Blantyre Newspapers Limited, 1985b).

Mzuzu's population trends past and present

As mentioned above, Mzuzu is now the third largest urban settlement in Malawi. The 1998 population and housing census reported a population of 87 030 people with an intercensal growth rate of 6.2 percent between 1987 and 1998. The population of 87 030 people represented 0.9 percent of the total population of Malawi at the time. Past population patterns reveal significant and progressive change in the population of Mzuzu as compared to other urban centres, in particular Zomba which Mzuzu surpassed between 1987 and 1998 in urban hierarchy on the basis of population size (Table 4.4). Actual population distributions for Mzuzu are outlined in Table 3.1. This data is according to the 1998 population census.

Table 3.1 Population of Mzuzu by ward

No.	Ward/Area	Households	Population
1	Chasefu	275	1 596
2	Chibanja	1 490	6 440
3	Chiputula	3 617	15 867
4	Jombo	244	1 333
5	Kaning'ina	646	3 701
6	Katoto	715	3 902
7	Katawa	610	2 876
8	Lupaso	2 169	10 084
9	Masasa	235	1 175
10	Mchngautuwa	3 742	16 112
11	Msongwe	268	1 540
12	Muzilawayingwe	603	2 779
13	New Airport Site	731	3 733
14	Nkhorongo	465	2 385
15	Viphya	1 427	6 752
16	Zolozolo	1 370	6 687
	Total	**18 607**	**86 962**

Source: Benson, T. (2002) *Malawi: an atlas of social statistics*

The National Statistical Office (NSO) population projections based on the 1998 population and housing census also show that the population of Mzuzu will be 175 061 by 2010 (Table 3.2). However, projections by the United Nations (2003) of world urbanisation prospects put the population of Mzuzu by 2010 lower at 148 000 (Table 4.7).

Table 3.2 Projected population of Mzuzu city (1998-2010)

Year	1998	2000	2002	2004	2006	2008	2010
Projected Population	87 030	99 095	112 535	126 885	142 129	158 204	175 016

Source: National Statistical Office (2002) *Malawi population and housing census*. Analytical report, 1998 Census

Notwithstanding the disagreement in projections, any further growth in population implies greater demand for economic opportunities and social supporting services like education, health, water, and electricity. Without economic development, such needs are unlikely to be met without a reduction in mass welfare of the residents of the city. Apparently, Mzuzu city is lagging behind when compared to the cities of Blantyre and Lilongwe. As was the case at the time Mzuzu became a city, the entire northern region's industrial and commercial requirements are met by firms based either in Blantyre or Lilongwe. This scenario partly reflects historical development trends and the underlying economic and demographic structures that imply low level of demand. The challenge is that the people of Mzuzu and the entire northern region are economically burdened as compared to their counterparts in the central and southern regions (Blantyre Newspapers Limited, 1985b). Even with a relatively backward development infrastructure, Mzuzu plays and occupies a critical spatial as well as strategic economic position as a regional growth centre. It is apparent that a concentration of social and economic activities in Mzuzu is essential in various ways for the long term development perspective of the northern region and the nation at large. It is within this framework that the informal economy, bicycle taxi and handcart operators in particular should be situated.

From a regional planning and development perspective, growth points (towns, cities and major trading centres) play crucial roles in agricultural production and even more so in food distribution and marketing. Rondinelli (1988) argued that growth points stimulate and strengthen the economic and physical linkages between urban and rural activities. Growth points structure marketing networks through which agricultural commodities are collected, exchanged and distributed. Without growth points agricultural trade is restricted to periodic markets in which subsistence farmers exchange goods among themselves. Rondinelli emphasized that in the absence of viable growth centres, the incentive to increase production that comes with the ability of farmers and other producers to market their goods competitively is lost and agriculture cannot expand easily beyond subsistence level. As agricultural productivity increases and farming becomes more commercialized, it depends more heavily on inputs produced in cities and distributed to rural regions through market towns and smaller urban centres. Further, a rise in income from increased agricultural production creates internal demand for a wide range of household and consumer goods. Without access to the goods and services that growth points offer, there may be little incentive for farmers to increase their output. These arguments justify the designation of Mzuzu as a city and provide the impetus for improved targeting and concentration of infrastructure and social services in Mzuzu. Local efforts like the work of bicycle taxi and handcart operators are an integral component in this respect.

Investment in Mzuzu city as a growth point could support the process of economic growth in the North and facilitate interregional integration and equalisation since economic growth integrates all relevant aspects of development at regional and national level (Rondinelli, 1988). As the fastest growing urban centre in Malawi, Mzuzu is witnessing the return of Asian businessmen and the construction or opening up of new institutions such as Mzuzu University, Mzuzu Central Hospital, and Auction Floors for the tobacco industry. These and other initiatives have multiplier effects on the economy and development of Mzuzu. However, in the *Nation Newspaper*, a journalist described Mzuzu city's townships as growing urban villages. In some of the features that caught the imagination of this reporter were scenes of barefoot children in tattered clothes, women drawing water from boreholes or wells close to streams in Ching'ambo, and bicycle taxis parked all over (Phiri, 2007). These images reflect high levels of poverty, with many of the poor categorized as ultra poor (Table 3.3).

Table 3.3 Poverty levels in Mzuzu city and other wards

Ward	Poverty headcount	Ultra poverty headcount
Mzuzu city	63.4	33.0
Chibanja	60.0	28.6
Chiputula	56.4	25.9
Kaning'ina	57.0	23.3
Katawa	43.2	16.9
Katoto	62.5	31.7
Lupaso	76.1	48.1
Mchengautuwa	61.3	29.6
Muzilawayingwe	61.9	29.1
New Airport site	84.7	57.8
Viphya	72.7	41.1
Zolozolo	58.1	26.8

Source: Benson, T. (2002) *Malawi: An atlas of social statistics*, p. 89.

Poverty is a symptom of urbanisation in Mzuzu, characterized by underdeveloped transport, health and education facilities as well as limited access to economic opportunities. Lack of employment and adequate housing leads to overcrowding, which comes with its own set of social and health problems (IRIN, 2004).

Conclusion

In this chapter I have situated the study in terms of geographic location, historical contexts, and national and local economic and social realities. I have also sketched the development prospects of Mzuzu city which is slowly becoming the hub of international or cross-border informal trade with Tanzania, with a role to play in regional and national development.

As young people continue to leave rural areas in search of employment, it is important to understand the processes of urbanisation and socio-economic development in specific localities. Increased investment in Malawi's rural areas is needed to keep people profitably employed on the land and thus stem rapid urbanisation. The next chapter seeks to paint the picture of the magnitude of urbanisation in Malawi.

Chapter Four

URBANISATION IN MALAWI

This chapter provides an overview of the process and state of urbanisation in Malawi which date only back to the late 19th century. Before, the entire length and breadth of Malawi was rural landscape. The only towns known prior to encounters with colonists were located along the lakeshore. These were Nkhotakota in the Centre and Karonga in the North. These towns developed into slave trade outposts for the East African slave trade that had its centre in Zanzibar. The Jumbe family in Nkhotakota and the Arab trader Mlozi in Karonga heralded the growth of these pre-colonial towns.

This chapter is not about the history of urbanisation but urban development in Malawi. A general overview of the process of urban development in Malawi is followed by a discussion of the characteristics of urbanisation in the post-colonial period. The chapter concludes with a look at the economic prospects of Mzuzu as an emerging city and the site of this study.

Urban development in Malawi

Malawi boasts of four main urban centres. The first to get established were Blantyre and Zomba in the south in the late 19th and early 20th centuries. The 1920s witnessed the sprouting of Lilongwe in the central region, which was later elevated to the status of the capital city. Much later in the 1940s Mzuzu was established in the North. Blantyre, Lilongwe and Mzuzu are designated as cities while Zomba is a municipality. There are eight towns namely: Karonga in the North; Dedza, Kasungu and Salima in the Centre; and Balaka, Liwonde, Luchenza, and Mangochi in the South (Table 4.1). Nkhotakota is not designated as a town, though its status as a district headquarters places it among the urban centres (Republic of Malawi, 1987). As is the case in other African countries like Egypt and Zimbabwe, all administrative centres in Malawi are regarded as urban areas. Therefore, all the district administrative headquarters or BOMAs are urban centres by virtue of their position as centres of government activities at the district level (Republic of Malawi, 1987).

Table 4.1 Cities, municipalities and towns in Malawi and their populations

Name	Region	1977	1987	1998	2003
Balaka	South		9 064	14 298	
Blantyre	South	222 153	333 120	502 053	646 235
Dedza	Central	5 448	16 899	15 408	
Karonga	North	11 873	19 667	27 811	
Kasungu	Central		11 591	27 754	
Lilongwe	Central	102 924	223 318	440 471	597 619
Liwonde	South		8 694	15 701	
Mangochi	South	3 341	14 758	26 570	
Mzuzu	North		51 904	86 980	119 592
Salima	Central	4 646	10 606	20 355	
Zomba	South	24 234	43 250	65 915	90 325

Source: Brinkhoff, T. (2003) Tables of towns of Malawi
www.citypopulation.de/Malawi.html

According to the United Nations, Malawi is one of the fastest urbanizing countries in the world (Table 4.2). Urban population has been growing at an annual rate of 4.6 percent per annum against the national average population growth of 2.9 percent in the 1970s, 3.2 percent in the 1980s and 2.0 percent in the 1990s. It is estimated that by 2015, 44 percent of the 11 million people living in Malawi in 2004 will be urban dwellers (United Nations, 2004).

Table 4.2 Urban populations ('000) (1950-2030)

Year	1950	1960	1970	1980	1990	2000	2010	2020	2030
Urban population	101	155	273	562	1 092	1 764	2 973	4 887	7 63ₐ

Source: United Nations (2007) *World urbanization prospects.*
http://esa.un.org/unup/p2k0data.asp

This is phenomenal growth compared to the period between 1966 and 1998 when the urban population rose from just 5 percent to 14 percent of the total population (Table 4.3).

Table 4.3 Urbanisation in Malawi (1966-1998), percentage of total population

Year	1966	1977	1987	1998
Rural	95.0	91.5	89.0	86.0
Urban	5.0	8.5	11.0	14.0

Source: Republic of Malawi, 1998

In the next few years, urban population is expected to grow at a rate of 6.3 percent per annum as compared to 0.5 percent in rural areas. The prime mover of urbanisation has been rural-urban migration, as more and more people from rural areas trek to towns and cities in search of better economic opportunities (Republic of Malawi, 1998).

The distribution of urban population is changing. In 1966 almost 70 percent of the urban population in Malawi lived in Blantyre. By 1977 the percentage dropped to 61 percent and at the moment it is only at 30 percent. By 1987, Mzuzu city had overtaken Zomba in the urban hierarchy (Table 4.4).

Table 4.4 Urban population ('000) in the four main urban centres (1966-2001)

Urban centre	1966	1977	1987	1998	2001*
Blantyre	109	219	333	479	503
Lilongwe	19	99	223	436	457
Mzuzu	8	16	44	87	91
Zomba	20	24	43	64	-

Source: Republic of Malawi, Population Census, 1977, 1998
* Economist Intelligence Unit (2001) *Malawi: country profile*, p. 3.

Table 4.4 reveals that Mzuzu and Lilongwe are growing even faster. Between 1987 and 1998 Lilongwe and Mzuzu grew by between 95 and 97 percent, while Blantyre and Zomba grew by 43 and 48 percent during the same period.

Characteristics of urbanisation in Malawi

Urban population change is commonly described by two measures: the level of urbanisation and the rate of urban growth.

The level of urbanisation is the share of a country's total population that lives in urban areas. The level of urbanization in Malawi hovered at 14 percent in 1998 and is rising mainly due to a large pool of potential migrants living in the countryside. Meanwhile natural population increase contributes significantly to the rate of urban growth. At this stage, seven points are particularly noteworthy. First, because urbanisation has resulted from rational economic decisions of migrants, urban growth and in particular rural-urban migration in Malawi should be perceived as more of an indication of the continued importance of migration in Malawi's economy than permanent urbanisation (Englund, 2002). This view is also supported by research. A study on street vending in Blantyre noted that 89 percent of the respondents were not born in Blantyre having migrated from the rural districts chiefly for economic reasons (Jimu, 2003). The study revealed that a majority of the street vendors came from the surrounding districts: Mulanje (18 percent), Nsanje (13 percent), Chiradzulu (12 percent), Thyolo (11 percent) and Zomba (9 percent). Only 7 percent of the street vendors came from outside the southern region districts of Ntcheu (5 percent), Dedza (1 percent) and Kasungu (1 percent). None of the street vendors interviewed came from the northern region of Malawi. Although these figures cannot be generalized to all populations of migrants, it is clear that rural-urban migration is propelled largely by economic reasons.

Second, although the rate of urbanisation in Malawi is on the increase, in 1996 it was far below the average rate of 30 percent for the sub Saharan Africa region (Table 4.5).

Table 4.5 Urbanisation rate in selected African countries (1980-1996)

Country	1980	1985	1990	1995	1996
Malawi	9.1	10.4	11.8	13.5	13.88
Kenya	16.1	19.8	24.1	28.6	29.5
Botswana	15.1	25.2	41.5	60.0	62.72
Ghana	31.2	32.3	33.9	35.9	36.4
Mozambique	13.1	19.8	26.6	33.8	35.08
Swaziland	17.8	21.8	26.4	31.1	21.02
Tanzania	14.8	17.6	20.6	24.2	24.92
Zambia	39.8	40.9	42.0	43.0	43.4
Zimbabwe	22.3	25.2	28.4	31.8	32.5

Source: Kaul and Tomaselli-Moschovitis, (1999): 117-8

These statistics are to be treated with caution. The definition of an urban population varies widely from country to country. Despite the notable variations in definition, the United Nations accepts each country's definition when it calculates urban population estimates and projections on the assumption that governments know best what features distinguish urban from rural places in their own countries. However, lack of standardized definitions hampers comparison of urban population data across countries as does the tendency among countries to change the definitions of urban places over time. In practice, this makes measurement of urban populations problematic.

Third, Kalipeni (1993) observed that prior to independence in 1964, urban population concentration was in favour of the southern region of the country and Blantyre in particular, the country's primary city then. Government's efforts to encourage population redistribution are yielding positive results. The demographic trend appears to have reversed in favour of the central and northern regions (Table 4.6). One notable effect of the policy initiatives is the growth of Lilongwe as a capital city and Mzuzu as the regional administrative centre for the North. Mzuzu is at the moment at the same level as Blantyre and Lilongwe in the urban hierarchy as national cities with growing international appeal and growing populations of immigrants from other African countries and Asia. Mzuzu and Karonga have substantial populations of Tanzanians while Blantyre and Lilongwe have sizable populations of Chinese, Lebanese, Nigerians, Zambians and Zimbabweans.

Table 4.6 Regional distribution of population in Malawi ('000 000) (1966-1998)

Region	1966	1977	1987	1998
Malawi	4.0	5.5	8.0	9.8
Northern region	0.5	0.6	0.9	1.2
Central region	1.4	2.1	3.1	4.0
Southern region	2.1	2.8	4.0	4.6

Source: Republic of Malawi (2003) Malawi in Figures 2000.

The pattern depicted in Table 4.6 is likely to change with the passage of time. It is anticipated that Lilongwe will surpass Blantyre by 2015 (Table 4.7). This is likely to happen since Lilongwe is by all accounts growing at a higher pace. As Douglas (2000) informs us, a map produced in 1895 of what is now Malawi showed Blantyre as the country's major settlement, far bigger than Zomba which was designated the country's capital in the 1890s. On this map Lilongwe and Mzuzu are not shown at all. At that point in history, Blantyre was an important town when Johannesburg, Nairobi, Lusaka and Harare were unimportant villages (Douglas, 2000). What other researchers have pointed out as Lilongwe's exorbitant growth rates in the 1970s due to urban-rural boundary changes (Englund, 2002) in the course of its establishment as the capital city needs revision in the light of continued momentum. Projections of future growth of the major urban centres suggest that Mzuzu city will remain for the foreseeable future the third largest urban settlement in Malawi (Table 4.7).

Table 4.7 Past and future urbanisation trends in terms of population ('000)

City	1950	1955	1960	1965	1970	1975	1980	1985	1990	1995	2000	2005	2010	2015
Blantyre	14	27	50	95	140	191	246	304	370	446	538	647	785	961
Lilongwe	2	4	8	17	32	64	112	181	266	362	493	655	842	1056
Mzuzu	1	1	2	4	7	12	22	40	59	75	95	119	148	185

Source: United Nations (2003) World urbanization prospects.
http://esa.un.org/unup

The fourth point is the proliferation of "urban villages" or rapid growth of rural settlements. Urban villages are characterized by a deplorable lack of the most basic requirements for a decent standard of living. Englund (2002) refers to Chinsapo in Lilongwe as a typical urban village in the capital city. In Blantyre, Kachere, Ndirande, Nkolokoti and Mbayani are typical cases. While in Mzuzu, Ching'ambo, Chibavi, Mtchengautuwa and Masasa fall in this category. Urban villages are known for unplanned and informal housing units at high density where most inhabitants are generally low income earners. Although the under performance of public utility companies affects all residential areas, those living in low income areas experience serious problems related to water and supply.

Fifth, the pattern of urban development and in particular the economic structures also reflect the temporality of urbanisation. In Malawi's urban areas it is not strange to hear people asking each other about their home and the answer is expected to include name of district, chieftaincy and possibly the name of the village. Englund (2002) noted in Chinsapo, Lilongwe that a stranger is likely to be asked, *kodi kuMudzi ndi kuti?*, which translates literally to 'where do you come from?' Englund uses this common practice to illustrate the temporality and transitory nature of rural-urban migration and residence among those who migrate and live in urban areas. As he argued, *Mudzi* translates not only as 'village' but also as 'home,' the ultimate 'our place,' an idiom imbued with affection and moral sentiments. The city is rarely thought to provide an adequate place of belonging such that rural-urban migrants identify themselves with the rural village from which they come and therefore belong even in situations from whence they have been away for long periods.

In addition, owing to low industrial development and historical economic inequalities , the retail sector is very small because of the limited purchasing power of the population. Urban centres are characterized by numerous small shops selling fabrics, shoes, basic stationary and imported electrical devices. Most of the shops are largely owned and run by Malawi's minority Asian population. Asian owned businesses are almost non-existent in rural areas following the tide on the African continent in the 1970s when a number of African countries took measures against Asians. The Malawi government forced the Indian population trading and living in rural areas to sell their houses and farms and to confine their economic activities and their residence to at first three and later four of the largest towns mentioned above (Pryor, 1990: 27). Hence, the retail business in the three cities and the municipality of Zomba is dominated by Asians. The Asian business community controls a disproportionate share, about 30 percent, of Malawi's total economy (Economic Intelligence Unit, 1997-8). Until the late 1990s, no natives had retail shops in the central business districts of Blantyre, Lilongwe and Zomba, hence the common rhetoric or mentality of *dziko ndi wanu koma ndalama ndi wanthu* (literally translated as: you own the country or you control the government, but we are in control over the economy) attributed to some people from the Asian business community.

Finally, the level of transport development is limited. Walking is the most common means of travel in both rural and urban areas. According to Kawonga (2006), short work trips are made within residential areas, but journey to work, school, and places for services, shopping, etc. generally involve longer walk trips. Kawonga further estimated that probably between 50 and 70 percent of workers in the low income group walk to work and a significant number walk long distances of about 3 to 5 km. He also notes that virtually all Malawian school children walk to school and it has been estimated that in Blantyre about 25 percent of them have a journey in excess of 2 km. Among the low income households, cycling is an important means of travel in both urban and rural areas. Kawonga further reported that close to 4 percent of head-of-household workers in low-income housing areas in Lilongwe use bicycles to travel to work. The proportion is estimated to be even higher for low income workers in Blantyre, which is regarded as Malawi's capital and Mzuzu, which is the third largest urban centre. The bicycle appears a very versatile means of transport, used extensively to convey relatives, produce and household goods. The real challenge is that road design does not allow for efficient cycling in cities and cyclists are often victims of road accidents. Another challenge is that there is no provision for parking of bicycles in public places (Kawonga, 2006).

Conclusion

The prevailing rate of urban growth in Mzuzu is not commensurate with the growth of the formal economy, and the situation has worsened over the last 10 years. Critics note that Malawi has become poorer since the reintroduction of multiparty democracy. The proliferation of the informal economy and the fact that 65 percent of the population lives below the poverty datum line of US$1 a day (Phiri, 2004) confirms the grave economic situation. The UN-Habitat has noted that the influx of people from rural areas to urban centres is directly linked to the increasingly harsh conditions many families are experiencing in the countryside (United Nations, 2004). Due to factors such as declining land-people ratios, falling soil fertility, and rising costs of farm inputs, it is no longer profitable for some families to continue with agriculture. Many young people leave rural areas in search of employment in towns and cities, yet migrating does not mean an end to poverty as employment opportunities in towns are not guaranteed. Poverty is actually increasing in urban households due to urbanisation. At the present rate of urban growth, the formal economy cannot absorb all the new job seekers. The real challenge is that urbanisation cannot be stopped whether by law, policy or development projects targeting the poor (Phiri, 2004). The informal economy offers hope though in most cases most of the jobs as shown in chapter two are low level and often unrewarding, as evidenced in this and subsequent chapters by the lives of bicycle taxi and wheelbarrow operators.

Chapter Five

THE URBAN INFORMAL ECONOMY IN MALAWI

This chapter provides an overview of the structure of the informal economy in Malawi and how it is intricately woven into the economic and social dynamics of life in the towns and cities of Malawi. My focus is on a number of recent changes, especially those with far reaching effects on the pace of growth of informality in economic circles. These include population growth and the adoption of accelerated or enhanced economic liberalisation policies. Despite shifts in economic policy emphasis from growth to poverty reduction and recently to growth and development, and transition from on party rule or dictatorship to multiparty democracy, the underlying causes of poverty are not addressed. Since the mid 1990s, the informal economy has been growing, as a grassroots adjustment to glaring and worsening poverty. Understanding its magnitude and characteristics is a first step in turning a developmental challenge into an opportunity.

Magnitude and characteristics of the informal economy in Malawi

The magnitude of the informal economy in Malawi is a matter of speculation because no comprehensive study has so far been accomplished. Various small scale studies however provide insight. A survey of 2 022 low-income households in the early 1990s found that 30 percent and 22 percent of the households in Lilongwe and Blantyre, respectively, were involved in informal economy activities (Chilowa, 1991 quoted in Green and Baden, 1994). The survey noted that many of the activities undertaken were casual and seasonal and often carried on alongside a range of other livelihood activities. A baseline survey by the Blantyre Urban Structure Plan team estimated the existence of 3 900 informal traders in the city in 1999. This was however a serious undercount and under representation of the real situation. Nevertheless, the baseline survey report noted that trading and vending were the main informal activity. The actors were involved in selling shoes, groceries and hardware items, cooked and uncooked foods, fruits and vegetables, used clothes imported from the west and motor spare parts. Most of the goods were imported from Zimbabwe and South Africa (Blantyre City Assembly, 2000).

The informal economy in Malawi is largely subsistence in nature. The Ministry of Economic Planning and Development (Republic of Malawi 1995:36) in the policy framework for poverty alleviation programme identified two characteristics that suggest that the informal economy is mostly subsistence in nature:
a) production of goods and services aims at generating incomes and employment for the beneficiaries;
b) businesses are labour intensive, use simple tools and technologies, and are seldom registered or licensed.

The informal economy expanded following market liberalisation in the 1990s. Orr and Orr (2002) indicated that between 1992 and 1999, the number of informal economy enterprise start-ups rose fivefold from 20 000 to 100 000.

Although the amount of income generated in the informal economy is hard to estimate, Orr and Orr (2002) noted that the share of income from informal economy enterprises is highest in the southern region of Malawi, with informal cross-border trade as one of the significant components (Minde and Nakhumwa, 1998), accounting for between 30 and 50 percent of wholesale turn over in the region in the 1990s (Whiteside, 1998). Malawi was the main source of manufactured goods for populations in the three Mozambique provinces of Nampula, Zambezia and Tete, while informal imports from Mozambique consisted largely of agricultural commodities (Minde and Nakhumwa, 1998).

The Malawi poverty reduction strategy paper (MPRSP) underscores the importance of informal economy or small to medium economic enterprises (SMEEs) as a tool to enable the poor to generate their own incomes. The GEMINI survey of 2000 estimated the existence of 747 363 micro small and medium enterprises (MSMEs) most of which were in rural areas. The survey noted that about 75 percent of MSMEs were off-farm activities involving manufacturing, commerce and trade, and services. The remaining MSMEs were involved in crop production (22 percent) and other primary activities (3 percent) such as livestock production, fishing, forestry and mining. About 91 percent of MSMEs were micro in size employing between 0 and 4 people. About 34 percent were owned by women, a proportion significantly lower than the average of between 60 and 75 percent recorded in most other African countries. Women's MSMEs were concentrated in off-farm commerce and vending of farm produce. Others were involved in manufacturing, in particular in processing of foods and brewing of beer (Republic of Malawi 2002).

The GEMINI micro and small enterprise baseline survey further observed that women accounted for 42 percent of total employment in the informal economy (Republic of Malawi, 2000b). This implied predominance of men as is the case in formal employment. This does not however imply that there are fewer poor females and female-headed households than poor men and men-headed households. The poverty analysis of the integrated household survey of 2000 showed that for every 100 women living in poverty in Malawi there are only 93.3 men in poverty. In non-poor households there are slightly more men than women (Republic of Malawi 2000a). Men head 75 percent of the total number of families and 72.6 percent of poor households. This implies that female-headed households are disproportionately poor. (Republic of Malawi, 2000a). The implication is that fewer women and female headed houses were involved in the running of informal economy businesses.

Although national statistics exclude the informal economy, because it is difficult to measure and little effort has been made to study its dynamics, it is generally acknowledged that most of those who are poor are involved in informal sector activities (Republic of Malawi, 1995: 36). Estimates by the National Statistical Office (NSO) indicate that the informal sector contributed income to 25 percent of Malawian households, employing 1.7 million people and generating 15.6 percent of GDP (Republic of Malawi, 2000c). In rural areas, it is the non-poor (people with access to capital) who own informal businesses while in urban areas it is the poor (Republic of Malawi, 2000a).

The informal economy is heavily constrained by factors like limited access to credit, lack of business management skills and technical know-how, lack of suitable premises, stiff competition from large firms and among informal entrepreneurs themselves, policy and legislative obstacles and severe market limitations (Republic of Malawi, 1995). The effect of these constraints were reflected in a survey of 26 000 enterprises in 2000 by the National Statistical Office which found that 80 percent of informal businesses were either stagnant or declining (Republic of Malawi, 2000b).

Rural-urban differences in informal economy activities

The place of residence, rural or urban, has an important bearing on poverty levels as well as the prospects and performance of informal economy businesses. The incidence of poverty is 10 percent less in urban areas than in rural areas (Republic of Malawi, 2000a). At the same time 47 percent of the population 10 years or older in urban areas is economically active as opposed to 70 percent in rural areas, mostly as smallholder farmers (National Statistical Office, 2002). In rural areas, non-poor households (25.2 percent) engage in non-farm business activities to a greater degree than the poor (20.2 percent). In urban areas however, 10 percent more poor households than non-poor households operate informal economy businesses (Republic of Malawi, 2000c). Trade is the dominant form of informal economy activities in both rural and urban areas. Yet, in rural areas it is the non-poor who have such businesses because they have sufficient capital to cover the costs. In urban areas street vending is a common activity and according to the Republic of Malawi (2000c) it is the poor who are the vendors. Most of the trade of the urban poor is small scale. The mean monthly sales revenues for the non-poor urban traders were 25-fold higher than those of the poor (Republic of Malawi 2000c). However, despite the importance of the informal economy – non-agricultural or off-farm activities as it is called in rural areas – most rural enterprises can best be described as income-generating activities that rarely develop into either stable or growth enterprises (Orr and Orr 2002). Orr and Orr (2002:8) further argue that 'most rural enterprises are unspecialized involving one or two people, carried out at or near the home, and operating for about eight months each year in order to fit in with agricultural activities and the need to secure household food supply'.

Factors that have shaped the structure and evolution of the informal economy

The informal economy in Malawi – the urban informal economy in particular – has been shaped by numerous factors including population dynamics, urbanisation, and economic and political changes over the years, as discussed below. As we will see, the accelerated economic liberalisation of the mid 1990s played an important catalytic role.

Population dynamics

Malawi is one of the densely populated countries in southern Africa. Malawi's population growth rate, currently at 3.2 percent. is one of the highest in the world. This high rate is due to a number of factors such as early marriages for women, a high and stable fertility rate of 6.7 births per woman, and a low percentage of families practicing child spacing partly due to low uptake of contraceptives. The crude death rate declined slowly from 25 in 1977 to 19 per 1 000 in 1987. The total fertility rate decreased from 7.6 in 1977, to 7.4 in 1987 and down to 6.7 in 1992. Although infant and child mortality rates have dropped to 16 and 26 percent respectively, they are still among the highest in the world. Table 5.1 is a summary of population growth patterns between 1901 and 1998.

Table 5.1 Malawi's population, growth rate and density (1901-1998)

Year	1901	1911	1921	1931	1945	1966	1977	1987	1998
Pop.	737153	970430	1201983	1573454	2049914	4039583	5547460	7988507	9933868
Growth rate	2.1	2.8	2.2	2.7	2.2	3.3	2.9	3.7	2.0
Density	7.8	10.3	12.8	16.7	21.9	43	59	85	104

Source: Republic of Malawi, 1998 Population Census

The average annual growth rate increased from 2.9 percent to 3.7 percent from 1977 to 1987 as a result of the influx of refugees from Mozambique. It is reported that at the peak of the influx there were over one million Mozambican refugees in the southern and central regions of Malawi. Malawi has a young population with 46 percent below 15 years of age. This implies a higher dependency ratio of 1.01 for each economically active adult. Apparently, the low level of literacy among females is one of the contributory factors to the high total fertility rate of about 6.7.

Socio-economic dynamics

Malawi is one of southern Africa's poorest nations with a per capita gross domestic product (GDP) of $210, average life expectancy of 38 years, national literacy averaging 22 percent, and high dependency on agriculture. Almost eighty percent of the population is unable to read and write, and 85 percent of the population lives in rural areas. Only 21 percent of women have received education beyond the primary school level. Over 70 percent of the population earns no income whatsoever indicating a high dependency ratio. The incidence of poverty is estimated at 60 percent of the total population in the early 1990s (Republic of Malawi, 1995) and 65.3 percent at the turn of the 21st century (Republic of Malawi, 2000d). Poverty is a problem in Malawi's four major urban centres of Blantyre, Lilongwe, Mzuzu and Zomba (Table 5.2).

Table 5.2 Poverty levels in four major urban centres

Ward	Poverty headcount	Ultra poverty headcount
Blantyre	62.9%	38.4%
Lilongwe	44.1%	19.9%
Mzuzu City	63.4%	33.0%
Zomba	70.1%	42.4%

Source: Benson, T. (2002) *Malawi: an atlas of social statistics*, pp. 89-92

Malawi has one of the lowest per capita incomes in the world (Table 5.3).

Table 5.3 Gross National Product (GNP) per capita in Malawi, US$ equivalent

Year	1978	1983	1988	1993	1998
GNP	180	210	170	200	200
Rank	16	8	6	9	7

Source: World Bank, 1980, 1985, 1990, 1997, 2000

Low income levels are partly a reflection of past historical developments. At independence in 1964 from Britain, the economy was rural based, characterized by three main sectors. First, the estate sector (large foreign-owned farms) produced 40 percent of the country's merchandise exports. Second, the smallholder sector (small indigenous-owned farms) produced for subsistence, but also provided marketed food surplus and export crops amounting to 50 percent of merchandise exports. Third, the labour reserve supplied estate labour and migrant labour to neighbouring countries (Harrigan, 2001; Humphrey, 1974; Pryor, 1990). Although there have been some efforts to diversify the economy, agriculture remains the mainstay of the economy, with over 75 percent of the population dependent on subsistence farming.

Despite almost four decades of independence, over which the government received financial and technical support from different donors (Harrigan, 2001), Malawi remains among the ten poorest countries in the world (Table 5.3) and is characterized by low levels of access to education. Only around 15 percent of the students attending primary school go on to secondary school and the dropout rate is 15 percent for girls and 20 percent for boys between 9 and 12 years of age. Life expectancy is at about 44 years, against the sub Saharan average of 52 years, and there is a high child mortality rate of 133 per 1 000 live births (Harrigan, 2001; Orr et al., 2001). A high percentage of households also suffer from food insecurity. Only 34 percent of the households meet the recommended daily requirements (RDR) of calories (Republic of Malawi, 2000a). Food insecurity is a pervasive phenomenon due to natural disasters (droughts and floods) but also high population densities, with the effect that average landholdings are too small to produce enough food for subsistence. Over the 2001-2002 periods, nearly 3 million out of a population of over 10 million (30 percent of the population) people suffered food insecurity (Devereux, 2002). The number of people in this situation rose to 4.5 million in the 2005-6 season. Improved food production in 2006-8 has seen the number of people dependent on food handouts reduced drastically. Yet, aggregate economic analyses indicate a deepening of poverty at the national level from 60 percent of the total population in 1990 to 65.3 percent in 1998 (Republic of Malawi, 2000b). The causes of poverty include poor economic policies and natural disasters. Poverty is growing despite a shift in economic policy from a 'growth strategy', with primary emphasis on estate agriculture (1964-1994), to a 'poverty alleviation' strategy, since 1994 (Economist Intelligence Unit (EIU), 2000; Harrigan, 2001). Malawi's poverty reduction strategy paper (PRSP) focuses on raising productivity and income of the rural poor with emphasis on smallholder agriculture, promoting private sector growth to expand non-farm employment, and improving and increasing social service provision (EIU, 1995-6). Over the years poverty has remained profound and widespread particularly amongst rural communities. Although poverty is more prevalent in rural than urban areas, income inequality is more severe in urban areas (Economic Intelligence Unit, 2002: 30).

Limited urban employment opportunities

Urban employment is largely based on a slow growing industrial base. Most industries are supply-based, processing agricultural products destined for export markets. There are a few demand-based or import substitution industries producing goods for the domestic market. Overall industry in Malawi is weak and highly dependent on South African and Zimbabwean manufacturers (Harrigan, 2001). The share of industry in the economy has grown slowly from 11 percent in the 1960s to 12.5 percent in the 1980s and 13.6 percent in 1998, and its share of formal employment has remained low at 15 percent of the total workforce in formal employment (Campbell, 2000: 171-176; Economist Intelligence Unit, 2002; Pryor, 1990: 44). Over the years total formal employment in both agriculture and the manufacturing industry has remained at less than 15 percent of the total labour force. The government has been the largest single employer of people in formal employment. For instance, the government employed 74 000 out of a total of 434 000 formal sector employees in 1986 of which 44.6 percent were skilled as compared to 26 and 10.7 percent in parastatals and the private sector (Republic of Malawi, 1994).

Low wages

Salaries for labourers and semi-skilled workers have always been low (Englund, 2002). Under one party rule, low wages were partly dictated by government's intervention in the pricing of goods and services which also necessitated a deliberate policy of depressed wage rates. The 1969 'National Wages and Salaries Policy' stipulated the need to keep wages very low. Between 1969 and 1981, wages declined in real terms by a factor of 34 to 40 percent, largely because of government imposed rigidity in money wages (Chipeta, 1990). Between 1984 and 1990 average monthly wage rates oscillated between US$34 and US$42 (Table 5.4). With economic liberalisation and problems related to data collection and accessibility, it has not been possible to provide information on changes in wage rates since then.

Table 5.4 Average monthly wage rates in Malawi Kwacha and US$ equivalent (1984-1990)

Year	1984	1985	1986	1987	1988	1989	1990
Wage	59.30	62.90	86.10	80.67	87.25	97.70	112.0
US$	42	34	37	37	34	35	41

Source: Economist Intelligence Unit (1986-1994) *Malawi: country profile*.

The effects of the low wage policy have not been remarkable as intended. The intention to encourage the establishment of labour-absorbing firms by keeping wage rates low has not been attained. Instead, economic liberalisation made technical advancement more important than economies relying on lower labour costs, hence the downsizing and closure of a number of firms since the mid-1990s, as elaborated in the subsequent section. The goal to promote agricultural development by discouraging rural-urban migration has not worked either. And plans to restrain domestic inflation and enhance Malawi's competitiveness in international markets flopped (Harrigan, 2001; Humphrey, 1974; Pryor, 1990: 158). An unintended consequence of the low wage situation, since at least the last years of the 1990s, is that industrial and commercial workers in urban areas have not been able to survive on incomes from wage employment. In rural areas, the situation has been compounded further by feudal relations of production whereby large numbers of estates and farms operate under quasi-feudal relations of wage labour combined with labour tenancy. Rapid expansion of the estate agricultural sector in the 1970s and 1980s failed to curtail rural-urban migration even though migration to towns and cities did not mean an end to poverty. Currently, a large percentage of urban residents live in misery and untold poverty. According to UNCHS, 71 percent of the residents of Blantyre live in unplanned settlements characterized by squalid living conditions. Poverty is pervasive throughout the city, with 65 percent of households living below the poverty line (IRIN 2004). Lack of employment and adequate housing leads to overcrowding, which comes with its own set of problems. These developments, though not properly explored in the Malawian context, have been observed in other African countries, for example Cameroon, to culminate in a situation whereby civil servants take on informal trading to supplement meagre incomes, termed 'straddling the formal and informal sectors' (Niger-Thomas, 2000).

In the case of most urban communities in Malawi, the tendency has been to engage in informal economy activities, trading in particular. For instance, in Blantyre Malawi's commercial centre unemployment rate in 1999 was estimated at 38 percent of the economically active population or 57.4 percent of the total population (Blantyre City Assembly, 2000). The Blantyre Urban Structure Plan team estimated that 46 percent of the households earned less than K 4 000.00 (US$ 43.00) per month. A breakdown of monthly household incomes in Malawi Kwacha, according to the housing density areas, indicated that average monthly incomes ranged from K 6 000.00 to K 34 000.00. However, such average incomes disguised wide disparities in income distribution, which were reported to be very high in Malawi's urban areas in the 1990s (Economist Intelligence Unit, 2002: 30). They also disguised the fact that some urban residents may not have an income of any sort as well as the irregularity of incomes among the unemployed, particularly those engaged in informal trading.

Structural Adjustment Policies (SAPs)

Some of the well known government structural adjustments of the 1980s and 1990s included reducing price controls in the domestic economy, raising prices paid to smallholder farmers to encourage more production, restructuring and privatising parastatals or statutory corporations, raising public utility rates to reduce deficits, increasing government revenues to reduce deficits in the public sector, and devaluing the currency (Economist Intelligence Unit, 1997-8). The socio-economic results of the SAPs have been bleak. Smallholder agriculture has not grown as fast as expected because of, among other factors including shortage of arable land due to high population density. A national sample survey of agriculture in 1992-93 showed that 78 percent of rural households had less than 1 ha of land as compared to the previous survey in 1985-86 which put the figure at 55 percent (Economist intelligence Unit, 2002). Lack of access to farm inputs worsened following removal of agricultural subsidies that made prices rise exorbitantly expensive. Worse still, the terms of trade on the international market declined (Orr et al., 2001). The restructuring and privatisation of statutory corporations starting from the late 1980s and intensified in the mid 1990s created acute job loses. For instance, the Press Holdings, a semi-state enterprise, had to lay off about 20 percent of its workforce in the 1980s and 1990s (Harrigan, 2001: 117).

Another notable feature of the late 1980s was the increase in redundancies in government and parastatal organisation. The process accelerated in the 1990s as the government struggled to keep the donors happy (Economist Intelligence Unit, 1995-6: 15-6). It is now evident that liberalisation of the economy in the 1990s also exposed local industries to stiff competition, which many were not mature enough to withstand. The Economist Intelligence Unit reported large job losses in manufacturing, of about 10.2 percent in 1981 and 11.6 percent in 1982, that were later counteracted by a 7.6 percent increase in employment in manufacturing in 1985 (Economic Intelligence Unit, 1987-8: 13). However, the enhanced liberalisation of the economy in the 1990s exposed local manufacturers to stiff competition from foreign goods and many failed to recover. According to Harrigan (2001: 2) Malawi is now in the process of de-industrialisation. While manufacturing grew by 3.3 percent per annum between 1987 and 1995, between 1996 and 1999 it stagnated and since then several industries have either stopped domestic production or closed completely.

The accelerated liberalisation of trade came with another dramatic economic change: inflation (Englund, 2002). The rate of inflation was 116 percent in 1994, 70 percent in 1996, and for most of the years up to 2002 it hovered at between 30 and 40 percent. Although the rate of inflation is now quite low, prices of most goods and services change frequently. Up against these developments, many households have had to find creative ways of earning income other than from formal employment and smallholder farming. They turned to activities within informal production and trading networks, activities perceived as essentially subsistence in nature (Republic of Malawi, 2000a). Characterisation of the informal economy as the bode of the unemployed, the poor, and the unskilled as well as largely dependent on family labour units and resources needs to be re-examined in the context of broader economic and political changes. The informal economy as we will see is integral and vital to the overall economy.

Urbanization, democratization and the informal economy

There is no single cause behind the proliferation of the informal economy in urban areas. Each of the dynamics discussed above has contributed. Lack of employment opportunities, low formal employment wage rates (Green and Baden, 1994), and changes in political and economic climate since the mid 1990s (Englund, 2002; Jimu, 2003) spurred rapid growth of the informal economy. Growth in urban population has not been accompanied by a commensurate growth in employment opportunities in commerce and industry (Jimu, 2003).

In studying the growth of street vending, Jimu (2003) observed that the remarkable proliferation of the informal economy in the 1990s coincided with political transformation from one party dictatorship to multiparty politics. Between 1964 and 1994, President Banda presided over a system that maintained legitimacy through 'astute combination of coercion, political patronage, and a populist appeal', which enabled him to define what constituted acceptable economic practices without any encumbrance (Economist Intelligence Unit, 1997-8; Englund, 2000: 582; Harrigan, 2001), hence 'bureaucratic denial of the existence of abject poverty in Malawi' (United Nations (1997), quoted in Harrigan, 2001: 31). The fact that the informal economy flourished even during autocratic rule implies the failure of the bureaucratic establishment to effectively implement laws and regulations. From the 1960s onwards, urban authorities with support from the police and the Malawi Young Pioneers used to apprehend the so called informal vendors. The highhandedness of law enforcement agents, however, failed to dissuade people from joining street vending. Many of the street vendors were beaten and their goods taken away without compensation. Although confiscation and beatings were popular in the 1980s and early 1990s, very few street vendors were prosecuted, convicted, fined or imprisoned. In most cases, the matter was settled amicably between the apprehended street vendor and his captor (Jimu 2003). The only recorded cases of conviction occurred in 1990 when about 80 street vendors in Blantyre were charged and fined K15.00 or sentenced to one month public works after being found guilty of hawking without a license, in violation of Blantyre City by-laws (Jimu 2003). The transition to multiparty politics opened opportunities for the assertion of rights. Englund (2000: 579) aptly described the situation:

> In most countries which experienced the 'second liberation' in the early 1990s, individuals and interest groups continue to feel entitled to assert themselves as bearers of rights, from the most inclusive human rights to more specific group rights.

The opening up of the economy created new opportunities for small-scale enterprises. As Englund (2002: 138) contends, the expansion of the informal economy and trading cannot be dissociated from the liberalisation of the economy which has, as he puts it, 'opened up new possibilities for small-scale entrepreneurship with no restrictions on spatial mobility within the country'. To crown the significance of liberalisation of both the economy and politics on the growth of the informal economy in Malawi, the former president Dr Bakili Muluzi acknowledged that liberalisation of the economy had opened opportunities to which the informal economy is a positive response in the following words: 'those who are doing small-scale business as vendors or hawkers are prospering in our liberalized economy' (Jimu 2003).

Conclusion

The size and structure of the informal economy in Malawi has been influenced by a myriad of factors such as population growth, rapid urbanisation, poor economic performance, and indirectly by accelerated economic liberalisation and the transition to multiparty politics. Understanding these factors and their interrelations helps us diagnosis challenges confronting the informal sector. It is within this framework that the bicycle taxi and handcart operators in Mzuzu should be situated. Urbanisation is not a mere increase in the population living and working in towns and cities, but a dynamic that in turn affects economic, demographic, political, cultural, technological and social changes. The extent to which different factors influence economic informality vary in time and space. The next two chapters focus on the social and economic characteristics of the bicycle taxi and handcart operators. The intention is to demonstrate how informal workers negotiate urbanisation thereby contributing to the construction and modification of urban socio-economic systems.

Chapter Six

INFORMALITY OF BICYCLE TAXIS AND HANDCARTS

Most studies of the informal economy have tended to focus on informality in retailing, wholesaling, crafts and manufacturing, while informality in the transport sector has received little attention, at least in southern Africa. The assumption has been that informality is less pronounced and hence insignificant in the transport sector. High levels of poverty, low level development of transport infrastructure and liberalisation of the transport sector in recent years set against the rising demand for mobility has complicated the transport landscape within and outside towns and cities of the developing world. This chapter looks at challenges of urban transportation in general and the development of bicycle taxi and handcart or wheelbarrow operations in Mzuzu.

Urbanisation and transportation

Transport supports mobility of passenger and freight and is important to urban life. Transportation in urban areas is complex because of the multitude of origins and destinations, and the amount and variety of traffic involved especially in big urban areas.

For the majority of people in many developing countries, walking is the most common means of transport, even for transporting goods. However, recent trends in transport development in developing countries show major increases in motor transportation (Button and Ndoh, 1991). Increasing affluence and desire for personal mobility contribute to this growth, especially in societies which have inadequate public transport systems. Button and Ndoh have noted that the growth in urban transport activity, coupled with rapid growth in urban population, results in intense road congestion leading to unproductive time delays and a lot of discomfort to the travelling public. Despite deregulation policies which have accelerated competition among passenger transport providers, resulting in wider participation of both motorized and non-motorized modes, problems of transport persist. Poor people are hardest hit, especially those that have settled on the outskirts of cities. Problems of connectivity compound already grave situations such as inadequate housing, sanitation and access to other facilities. In such circumstances transport is often provided by old, poorly maintained vehicles and characterized by long waiting times and overcrowding. Convenient non-motorized forms of transport are also available and contribute significantly to both the formal and informal economies.

Achieving an efficient and rationally functioning transport system is beset by numerous challenges. According to Rodrigue (2008), problems of urban transportation could be disaggregated into:

- Congestion, which is one of the most prevalent transport problems in large urban centres. Congestion is particularly linked with motorisation and the diffusion of the car, which has increased the demand for transport infrastructures.
- Since vehicles spend the majority of the time parked, motorisation has expanded the demand for parking space.
- Many public transit systems, or parts of them, are either over or under used. During peak hours, crowdedness creates discomfort for users, while low ridership makes many services financially unsustainable, particularly in suburban areas.
- Increased traffic has adverse impacts on public activities which once crowded the streets such as markets, parades and processions, games, and community interactions. More traffic impedes social interactions and street activities. People tend to walk and cycle less when traffic is high.
- Pollution, including noise, generated by circulation has become a serious impediment to the quality of life and even the health of urban populations.
- Energy consumption by urban transportation has dramatically increased and so the dependency on petroleum.
- Growing traffic in urban areas is also linked with a growing number of accidents and fatalities, especially in developing countries. As traffic increases, people feel less safe to use the streets.

Some of these challenges affect or are experienced by both the motorized and non-motorized transport operators in Malawi. In the city of Mzuzu, non-motorized transport operators include bicycle and handcart or wheelbarrow operators.

Overview of transportation in Mzuzu

Like other cities in the developing world, much of the transportation in Mzuzu takes place by road, ranging from walking on unpaved paths to motor transport (big buses, minibuses and conventional taxis) on unpaved and well paved roads. As we stated earlier, for the majority of people walking is the only option. According to Singini (undated), in the past young men could walk as far as 70 kilometres to deliver messages. People walked frequently to and from Ekwendeni, a Presbyterian mission station north of Mzuzu to buy salt from shops owned by Indians, Mandala and Kandodo.

Photo 6.1 Scene along one of the streets in Mzuzu city

Photo 6.2 Scene at Katoto filling station

Bicycle taxis and handcarts or wheelbarrows in Mzuzu

Bicycle taxis and handcarts or wheelbarrows, upon which the study that has inspired this book is centred, have different histories. A wheelbarrow is traditionally a farm implement used for ferrying farm inputs and outs. In the city of Mzuzu, wheelbarrows and their proto-types are widely used for transporting agricultural commodities, fish, bales of second clothes, timber and other merchandise.

Photo 6.3 Wheelbarrow operator outside the Mzuzu bus terminal
Handcarts and wheelbarrows are part and parcel of life in Mzuzu city, however their operators and the residents of Mzuzu do

not know their origin. As explained in the introductory chapter, the terms handcart and wheelbarrow are used interchangeably in this book to describe a single or double wheeled cart used to transport goods, as pictured in Photos 6.2 through 6.5. In essence, the term handcart is used loosely.

Photo 6.4 Two wheeled handcart loaded with planks for the carpentry shops in Luwinga

Photo 6.5 Wheelbarrows parked for the night on the veranda of a retail shop in Mzuzu

Bicycle taxis on the other hand are ordinary bicycles fitted with a comfortable seating pad at the back for the passenger. On the origin of bicycle taxis, credit is given to the innovativeness of a person known as Sata, who was at the time of the survey working as a shop assistant for an Indian family.

Photos 6.6 Bicycle taxi operators waiting for clients in Luwinga (above) and Katoto (below)

Photo 6.7 Bicycle taxi operator on the M1 (Mzuzu-Karonga road)
The story of Sata is a story of innovative negotiation of the
challenges of unemployment, low wages and alienation associated
with urbanisation in emerging cities of the developing world.

It is well known in Malawi that shop assistants work under sordid conditions that include low wages as well as dehumanizing racist treatment. In a bibliographic note in George Simeon Mwase's *Strike a Blow and Die: A Classic Story of the Chilembwe Rising* (1970), Robert T. Rotberg reported that the Central Province Native Association (formed in 1927) condemned Asians as the 'swindlers and maltreaters of Africans'. Most shop assistants in both formal and informal sectors are grossly underpaid. For those working for the Asian shopkeepers, wages are fixed so low on the pretext that local employees are untrustworthy and more likely to reward themselves through theft of merchandise and sometimes misappropriation of cash. There are always stringent measures meant to check and control unscrupulous employees from paying themselves handsomely through theft. Meanwhile employees regard low wage rates as a form of theft by employers (Englund, 2002). Faced with a choice between employment with low wages and unemployment with no wage, many young men chose work, but they have to complement the meagre earnings by straddling the shop assistantship with bicycle taxi operations, or any opportunity that may come their way to make ends meet. Niger-Thomas (2000) noted a similar situation in southern Cameroon. Considering the poor socio-economic standing of many informal as well as those at the very margins of the formal economy, the informal economy per se is a vital livelihood alternative of first as well as last resort. Those who join out of necessity are in the majority.

Life story of Sata

Sata, aged 29 at the time of the interview, comes from the central district of Lilongwe. Like most bicycle taxi operators, he is married with two children. He lives in Chibanja with his wife. The children are however living with their grandmother in Lilongwe. Sata is known to be the first person to experiment with the bicycle taxi business in Mzuzu city. He came to Mzuzu in 1991. Then he was employed as a shop assistant by X Shopping Centre in Lilongwe. He was transferred to their new shop in Mzuzu. He worked with X Shopping Centre in Mzuzu from 1991 to 2003. He left because his employers were not ready to increase his salary, on which he could hardly survive. The employer argued that he was not responsible for his specific problems, for example house rent. Then Sata was asked to resign for expressing dissatisfaction with his wages. He left the job and started selling sweets at Namizu. He was however recalled mid 2005 on the promise of a better salary. Sata recalls that income from the small business he had started was handsome. Yet, he felt he should diversify by starting a bicycle taxi business in early 2004. Although he was ridiculed, some encouraged him on the premise that the practice was already common in other places in Malawi. Initially, daily income was between K800.00 and K900.00. On bad days his income could be K700.00. His exploits attracted other operators. Although he has rejoined X Shopping Centre, Sata regards himself as a bicycle taxi operator. From Monday to Saturday, he works at X Shopping Centre from 8.00 am to 5.00 pm and then operates the bicycle taxi till 9.00 pm. He has two sources of income: his monthly wage as a shop assistant and the daily income from operating a bicycle taxi.

Opportunities for operators and organisation of operations

The tale of Sata illustrates self-employment and opportunity to earn relatively high incomes as discussed further in chapter 8. In his own words, Sata explained it like this:

> Some people laughed, while others encouraged me to continue with the service. Others encouraged me by saying that this practice is common in other places. I used to make a lot of money in a day. I was assured of getting between K800.00 and K900.00 in any single day. Even on bad days my income never went below K700.00. I was then joined by others.

The operators are organized in ranks, a rank being an operating base from where clients could access the service. Ranks are scattered throughout the city centre to different destinations. There is a lot of flexibility in terms of distances, fares and destinations. While most of the handcart operators do their work within Mzuzu, some bicycle taxi operators cover long distances to places like Rumphi Boma and Phwezi situated to the north and northwest of Mzuzu on the Mzuzu-Karonga road, though such long distance trips are rare.

Table 6.1 Notable ranks and destinations

Notable Ranks	Destinations within Mzuzu	Destinations Outside Mzuzu
Bus Depot Namizu Kandodo Shop Mzuzu Main Market Hardware Market Shoprite (SP 12) Katoto (KO-10) Chiputula Junction Mwizalero (MZ) H.H. Wholesale	Chibavi Chiputula/Mzilaingwe Katawa/Chasefu Masasa Zolozolo/Mary Mount Msongwe Luwinga Nkholongo Moyale Barracks Mzuzu Government School	Mzgola on the road to Biya Chigwere along Chikwina road Biya on the road to Usisya Kadikechi (K150.00) Choma Lusangazi/Malivenji Rumphi (round trip: K500.00) Phwezi (round trip: K800.00) Enyezini (K200.00) Chikwina

Photo 6.8 Scene at Matabwa market

Fares are relatively proportional to distance. In some cases the terrain is the most important consideration in determining fares. Other considerations are the size and nature of the load whenever commodities are involved. The size and nature of the load is particularly important for the handcart operators since their business is mainly to transport commodities. It was out of the ordinary to note that the socio-economic status of the clients is not an important factor in the calculation of fares. Different reasons were put across for not considering the socio-economic situation of individual clients. Some of the important points were:

- To be fair to everybody;
- Overcharging is stealing;
- Fares are determined by the association and so far socio-economic status of clients is not a criterion for determining fares. Similar findings are recorded in a report on cross border trade by Minde and Nakhumwa (1998). They noted that bicycle operators are organized into informal associations that settle disputes, determine new entrants into the business and collude in setting the bicycle hire charges;
- There is always room for bargaining or haggling. In research on street vending in Blantyre, Jimu (2003) noted that this

trait is an important feature of business in the informal sector. It is a mark of competitiveness.

As will be illustrated in the next chapter, it may be surmised that since the operators and most of the clients live in low income residential areas, there is a certain level of appreciation that hinges on better understanding of each others' respective income and economic situation. The few operators that mentioned taking into account the socio-economic situation of their respective clients when charging the fare noted that this is part of bargaining. Bargaining or haggling is one of the essential characteristics of business in the informal economy, whereby the motive is to get a good income as much as possible. Hence, there is nothing immoral.

Photo 6.9 Scene at Namizu depicting bicycle taxis waiting for clients

Photo 6.10 Heading to Chibavi township by bicycle taxi

Challenges faced by the operators

The operators reported many challenges. Some of them are in fact unfulfilled expectations, reflecting an inherent contradiction between the subjective aspirations and the objective situations of operators. Many challenges are simply a result of problems inherent to informality, such as lack of effective regulatory mechanisms. Some of these challenges were identified in the policy framework for poverty alleviation developed by the Ministry of Economic Planning a decade ago (Republic of Malawi, 1995). They include instability of income, traffic problems, competition, problems of organisation and other issues as follows:

- Instability of income: This problem is experienced by both bicycle taxi and handcart operators. Incomes fluctuate responding to cycles of household incomes and expenditure patterns. Incomes are high towards the end and at the beginning of the month. Incomes also fluctuate throughout the year. Festive seasons such as Christmas and New Year holidays happened to be the best times for business, especially for the bicycle taxi operators. The peak period is however the tobacco selling season, which runs from the end of March to August/September;

- Some clients do not appreciate the value of the service they get from the bicycle taxi and handcart operators. Such clients negotiate for low fares while others shun paying. This is particularly a problem for the bicycle taxi operators;

- Roads are narrow and the edges too dangerous to facilitate free flow of traffic (Photo 6.11). The result is congestion on the roads due to competition among vehicles, cyclists and pedestrians. Pedestrians insist on walking in the middle of the road. Some do not appreciate the need to give way to cyclists, especially the bicycle taxi operators. As noted in a focus group discussion with bicycle taxi owners, some pedestrians argue that they cannot give way to cyclists as they do to vehicles. In the case of handcart or wheelbarrow operators, especially those involved in the transportation of timber, there is always a problem of blocking free flow of vehicular, cyclist and pedestrian traffic;

- Stiff competition among bicycle and handcart operators as well as competition from minibus operators. This aspect contributes to instability of incomes and hostility or lack of harmony among the operators;

- Problems of organisation and cooperation among the bicycle operators: despite the existence of the Mzuzu Bicycle Operators Association (MBOA), some cyclists operate outside its regulatory framework. It is a requirement that all operators have identity cards, yet some do not. This situation weakens cooperation and is a recipe for competition, rather than cooperation. Although it is also required that all operators belong to specific ranks, some disregard these arrangements;

- Frequent road accidents involving mainly the bicycle taxi operators discourage some people from patronizing the service;

- Theft of bicycles by thugs who disguise themselves as clients;

- Frequent breakdowns that necessitate costly maintenance and repairs;

- Lack of security against sickness, which implies loss of income. Apparently, this is a common challenge experienced by workers in the informal economy regardless of whether they are employed or in self employment. There is no health insurance and income is not guaranteed;

▪ Limited access to credit particularly due to lack of collateral;

▪ Lack of business management skills and suitable business premises.

The similarity in the list of challenges indicates that government is not ignorant of the constraints confronting the informal economy. Rather, lack of attention implies lack of commitment among government officials at different levels from the local to the national government to institute strategies that can guarantee better business environments for the poor eking a living in the informal economy.

Photo 6.11 Gullies on edges of roads prevent bicycle taxis from giving way to other users

Accounts of accidents involving bicycle taxi operators

Bicycle taxi operators have been involved in several fatal accidents. In the last two years several pedestrians have been hit by bicycles and a handful of operators and their clients killed when bicycle taxis collided with vehicles. One Saturday morning a young woman in her twenties hired a bicycle taxi to take her to church to register for a marriage. On the way a truck carrying bales of tobacco from the auction floors tipped and crushed the bicycle operator and his female client to death. Another incident involved a prominent choir member and son of the catechist at one of the churches in Mzuzu. This client fell off on a tarmac road on his head and died instantly. Several other clients have been injured when bicycle taxi operators failed to brake and crashed into stationary vehicles or landed in drains by the roadside. Faulty brakes, speeding, ignorance of the Highway Code and negligence have been blamed for numerous accidents involving bicycle taxis.

Overcoming the challenges

Bicycle taxi and handcart operators deploy various tactics to negotiate and overcome some of the challenges. Although the approaches are numerous and varied in nature, they can be broadly categorized into three. These three approaches are by no means mutually exclusive.

First are individualized solutions to the problems. This category includes:

- Working long hours: Some work from dawn to dusk with a short break in between for a snack. The goal is to serve as many clients as possible. Some operators overwork themselves and fatigue is evident on their faces;
- Observing the traffic code to avoid accidents; as well as
- Being vigilant about the kind of clients one is serving. The desire is to avoid known cheats or people with doubtful identities.

The second category includes collective solutions such as:

- Joining Mzuzu Bicycle Operators Association (MBOA): The association is an umbrella body of the Mzuzu bicycle taxi operators. It was formed between January and February 2005 to regulate bicycle taxi operations through establishment of ranks and issuing of IDs; promote cooperation; mobilize social and financial support towards operators who are sick, injured in road accidents and bereaved; and serve as a forum through which the bicycle taxi operators could know each other and share experiences;

- Regulating competition by operating from established ranks only;
- Charging uniform fares, although this does not stop passengers from negotiating for or operators accepting low fares.

The last type of approach is working with the authorities including the traffic and public order police. The police have in the past organized meetings to brief bicycle taxi operators on traffic regulations. To facilitate easy identification of bicycle taxi operators, the Mzuzu Bicycle Operators Association (MBOA) was formed in 2004 and collaborated with the police to introduce identity cards for the bicycle taxi operators. However, the association does not have control over the issuing of IDs, the screening of recipients or the manner of issuing IDs. The production of the IDs is coordinated by a separate entity – the Mzuzu Youth Crime Prevention Forum, popularly known as the Forum. Currently a large number of the operators do not have IDs. Many operators consider the IDs as unnecessary paraphernalia and well beyond their means. The handcart operators do have ad hoc committees at each rank that regulate business specifically for that rank.

Conclusion

Informality in the transport sector is a product of society and the economy. Problems of poverty and needs for connectivity are negotiated by resorting to non-motorized forms of transport.

In this context, bicycle taxis and wheelbarrow operations provide self-employment and facilitate human interactions and commercial transactions. However, the operators are beset by numerous challenges including competition, instability of income, frequent road accidents some of which lead to death, lack of access to credit, and other forms of insecurity. Operators seek to overcome the challenges through individual ingenuity and cooperation among the operators and with the state and its agents.

Chapter Seven

SOCIAL ATTRIBUTES OF THE OPERATORS

This chapter focuses on who the bicycle taxi and handcart operators are, by exploring their social profile. The other major focus of the study, their economic profile, is covered in chapter 8. Findings regarding their social profile concur with observations in previous surveys on informality in Malawi, for example a study conducted in Blantyre in 2002 about the growth, dynamics and politics of street vending (Jimu, 2003) and a reconnaissance survey of social, economic and environmental impacts of street vending in Mzuzu city (Chirwa, 2000). The social profiles of informal economy workers are structured and formed by the nature of society and the economy. In the case of informality in Malawi, significant economic factors have been discussed in earlier chapters. In this chapter, summary findings are provided on the social ecology of the informal economy including socio-demographic factors such as age, gender, marital status, education level, and migration tendencies. From a social ecology perspective, the most notable observation however is related to place of residence and residential status in the city. It is known that informal or squatter settlements provide sanctuary to informal economy workers. As for bicycle taxi and handcart or wheelbarrow operators, most live in high density traditional housing areas (THA) where the provision of social amenities is hardly adequate.

Rural roots and transitory stay in the city

The bicycle taxi and handcart or wheelbarrow operators in Mzuzu reported coming from various rural districts of Malawi to which they hope to return at some point in their life. Migration to and residence in Mzuzu is seen in most cases as part of a lifestyle in which improvements in the rural homes are sought by a brief stay in the town or city. Rural-urban migration is socially as important as it was in the early years of independence when most of the internal migration was to the cities of Blantyre and Lilongwe.

Very few bicycle taxi and handcart operators in the sample have lived in Mzuzu city since birth, and very few have been living in Mzuzu for more than 10 years. Most of the operators are recent migrants from the rural districts in all three regions of Malawi.

However, it appears that a majority of the operators are from the North (Table 7.1).

Table 7.1 Home regions of the operators

Region	Number	Percent
North	35	87.5
Centre	3	7.5
South	2	5

Only five respondents reported coming from districts outside the northern region, representing 12.5 percent of the sample. The remaining 35 respondents came from within the North representing 87.5 percent of the sample. The sample also shows that Mzimba district commands a disproportionate share of the population involved in these activities. About 23 respondents indicated coming from Mzimba district, representing 57.5 percent. The remaining 12 respondents, representing 30 percent of the sample, came from other districts in the northern region (Figure 7.1).

Figure 7.1 Districts of origin of operators

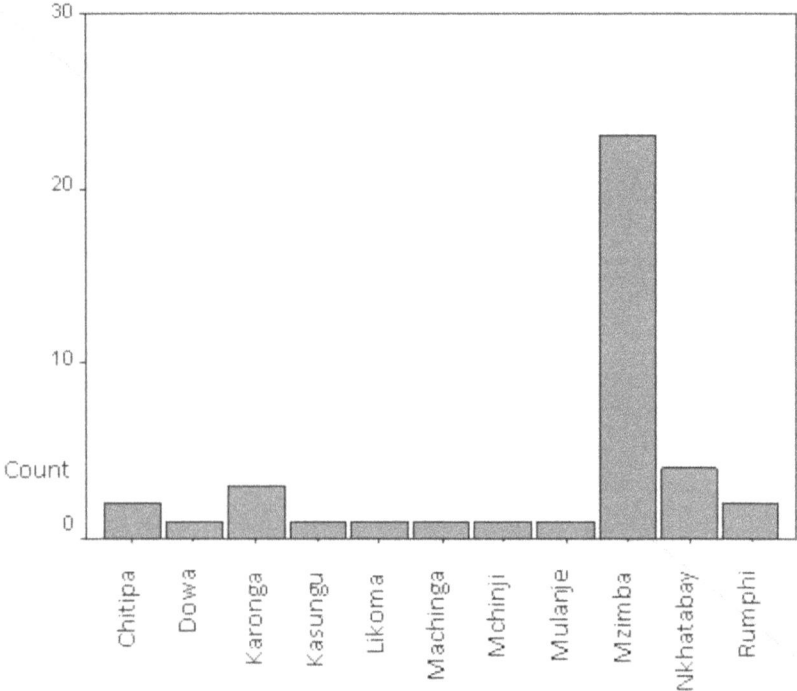

Data from the current survey is not comprehensive enough to warrant firm conclusions on the nature of rural-urban migration. Tentatively, if the overrepresentation of operators from Mzimba district is not due to a sampling error, proximity could be the explanation because Mzuzu is located in Mzimba district. Rural people make short and frequent journeys to neighbouring villages and urban residents to neighbouring townships. This suggests that migratory tendencies of informal economy workers tend to be restricted by distance. Alternatively, Mzimba happens to be the largest district of the six in the northern region of Malawi. Therefore, the overrepresentation of operators from Mzimba is nothing more than a reflection of the population as well as the economic dynamics of the region. Numerous studies have demonstrated that rural-urban migration is principally driven by economic motives (Kalipeni, 1993; Jimu, 2003). Therefore, there are good reasons for believing that most bicycle taxi and handcart operators came to Mzuzu to look for better economic opportunities (Figure 7.2). This point will be developed further in the next chapter on the economic profile of the bicycle taxi and handcart operators. Suffice it to say that the majority are involved in the informal economy partly because employment opportunities in the formal economy are hardly available in adequate quantities to absorb each and every job seeker. Apart from the majority of operators who came to Mzuzu to seek employment (70 percent), others have lived in Mzuzu city since birth (5 percent), while others came to live with relatives (17.5 percent) and only 1 operator representing 2.5 percent of the sample came to work as a bicycle taxi operator.

Figure 7.2 Motives for coming to Mzuzu

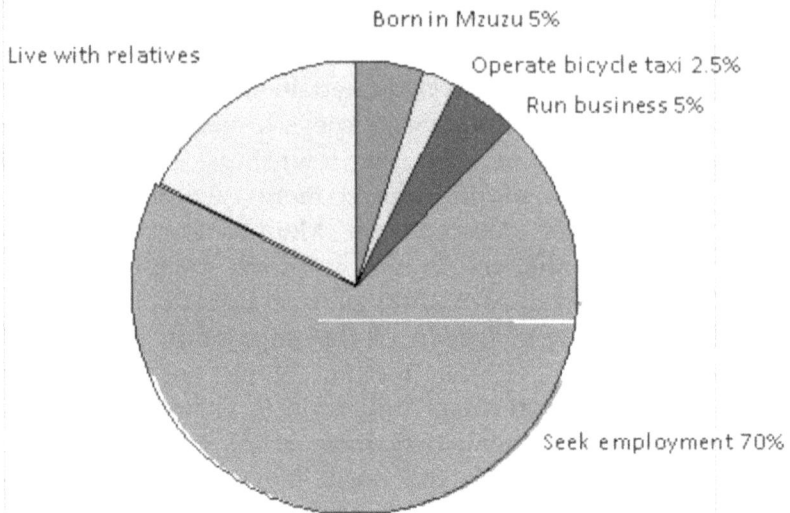

Born in Mzuzu 5%

Live with relatives

Operate bicycle taxi 2.5%

Run business 5%

Seek employment 70%

The fact that 77.5 percent of the operators interviewed cited reasons that are economic in nature for coming to Mzuzu, that is seek employment, do business or operate a bicycle taxi service (Figure 7.2), confirms that rural-urban migration in recent years represents the persistence of economic motives often alluded to in the literature on migratory tendencies in the late colonial and early post colonial periods. While in colonial times and the early years of independence migration to the mines and commercial farms in South Africa, Zambia and Zimbabwe was far more significant, since the mid 1970s to the early 1990s, rural to rural migration was encouraged and facilitated by the rapid expansion of the estate agricultural sector. However, the adoption of multiparty politics in 1994 and enhanced liberalisation of the economy described in chapter 5 presented enormous economic challenges but also possibilities for entrepreneurship with minimal restrictions on spatial mobility (Englund, 2002). It was in this context that migrants were coming to Mzuzu and migration persevered as a way by which people seek economic betterment. In most cases mobility is a lifestyle in which improvements in the village are pursued through a brief stay in town, indicating thus, as Englund further argued, the continuing importance of migration rather than permanent urbanisation. This is also supported by migration theories which show that the majority of migrants from rural areas move to cities in search of employment because urban wages are practically always higher than rural ones. Similarly, availability and quality of public services in towns and cities exceed that in rural areas and migrants seeking to improve their standards of living often believe their lives will be better of in the city. I have substantiated this argument in the next two chapters, in particular in chapter 8 with the life stories of selected bicycle taxi and handcart operators.

Set in the national context, results of the 1998 population census revealed higher poverty levels in rural than urban areas. However, the levels of poverty for the districts in the North do not support the conclusion that the rural-urban migration is due solely to higher levels of rural poverty. This is evident from Table 7.2. Poverty levels for Mzuzu city are higher at 63.5 percent as compared to the regional average of 61.1 percent. Mzimba district, from which most of the bicycle taxi and handcart operators come, has a poverty rating of 63.5 percent, which is about 0.3 lower than that of Mzuzu city. Lowest levels of poverty are for those of Karonga and Likoma Island at 48.5 and 52.5 respectively.

Table 7.2 Poverty levels in northern Malawi

District	Poverty headcount %
Northern region	61.1
Chitipa	66.6
Karonga	48.5
Likoma	52.5
Mzimba	63.2
Mzuzu city	63.5
Nkhata-Bay	60.2
Rumphi	66.6

Source: Benson, T. (2002) *Malawi: an atlas of social statistics.* p. 88

Socio-demographic characteristics of the operators

In terms of socio-demographic characteristics, most of the operators are young men in their 20s and 30s. There are few very young operators, and there is no operator who can be categorized as old by age. In terms of education attainment, most of the operators completed primary education but only a small percentage attended secondary school. These socio-demographic characteristics are typical of informal economy workers, except the overrepresentation of males noted in these two occupations as explained in subsequent sections.

Ages of the operators

There was no operator below 10 years of age. There was only one in the 10 through 19 age range and 18 in the 20 through 29 range. The majority (21) were 30 or older (Table 7.3).

Table 7.3 Ages of respondents

Age range	Frequency	Percent
10-19	1	2.5
20-29	18	45.0
30+	21	52.5
Total operators	40	100

The data shows that these activities are for the middle aged and the most productive age group or generation, in line with labour force segmentation in the informal economy whereby middle aged groups predominate in strenuous and labour intensive tasks. Cycling and pushing handcarts requires a lot of physical energy and resilience associated with youthful groups. As will be discussed in chapters 8 and 9, these tasks offer relatively better income opportunities than others in the informal economy.

Sex composition of the operators

In Malawi, sex ratio ranges from 96.1 to 105. According to Benson (2002) sex ratio compares the numbers of males to the number of females in the population. Equal numbers of each gender gives a sex ration of 100. In 1998, the sex ratio for Malawi was 96.1, which implies that there were just over 96 males for every 100 females. However, for most urban areas, males outnumbered females.

All the bicycle taxi and handcart operators in Mzuzu happen to be male. These activities are thus not a convenient space for studying dynamics of rural-urban migration because they do not reflect the rural-urban migration tendencies of women. The observation regarding the sex of participants is unique for two specific reasons. First, the informal economy in general has never been the abode of males only. Studies in Africa and other countries in the developing world have shown that women constitute the principal labour force in the informal sector, particularly in such activities as food and beverages, retail trade, pottery, basket weaving and cross border trade (Murry, 1991; Niger-Thomas, 2000; United Nations, 1996). A sectoral analysis of women's participation in the informal sector in the Congo, the Gambia and Zambia in the early 1990s indicated that women constituted 94.1, 88.9 and 90.6 percent of retailers, respectively (United Nations, 1996: 11). Even in apartheid South Africa, women constituted the majority of participants in the informal sector (Friedman and Hambridge, 1991). The dominance of female participants in the informal sector has been shown to be a factor of low education attainment and employable skill levels among women, which in a competitive labour economy preclude a majority of them from directly enjoying the benefits of a growing formal wage sector. Feminist analysis blames gender bias inherent in patriarchal societal arrangements for favouring males over females in education, skill training and employment. The second unique point is that there are no taboos against women cyclists. Indeed, there are some women cyclists in Mzuzu yet none is involved in the bicycle taxi and handcart operation businesses.

In terms of the sex of the clients patronizing bicycle taxis, it seems there is no discrimination along sex lines as the data in Table 7.4 illustrates.

Table 7.4 Sex of clients

Sex of most clients	Frequency	Percent
Female	8	20.0
Male	15	37.5
Both male and female	17	42.5
Total operators	40	100

Only 20 percent of the respondents indicated having more female clients, compared to 37.5 percent that claimed to serve more male clients against 42.5 whose clients are made up of equal numbers of males and females.

Marital status of the bicycle taxi and handcart operators

In the formative years of informal sector studies, critics viewed informal economy workers as petty commodity producers or traders (Dasgupta, 1973; Hart, 1973). It was then widely felt that they do not make any contribution to the economy. This survey noted that while it may be difficult to quantify the economic benefits, the social benefits are easier to appreciate since the bicycle taxi and wheelbarrow or handcart operators in Mzuzu, like all workers in the informal and the formal economy, have families that they support from the incomes or proceeds from informal self employment. There were three ways bicycle taxi and handcart operators described themselves in terms of marital status. Out of the 40 respondents, 26 representing 65 percent are married and have children. They support their families using the proceeds from the bicycle taxis and handcarts.

Figure 7.3 Marital status of the operators

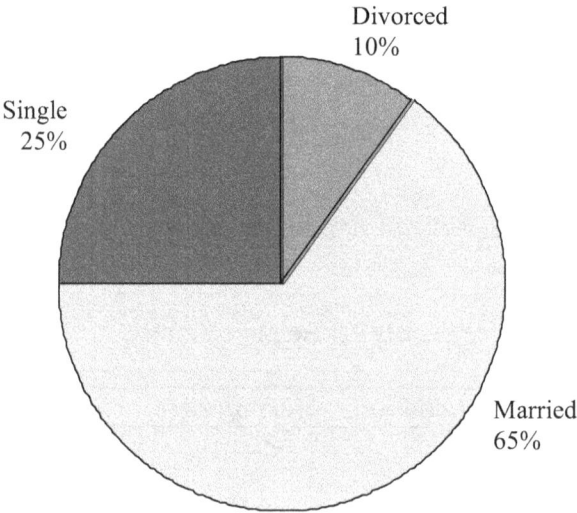

However, 25 percent of respondents are single (Figure 7.4). Even unmarried bicycle taxi and handcart operators indicated having dependants, usually younger siblings, cousins or nephews and nieces. Similarly, there are adult dependants (Table 7.5). Out of the 40 respondents, 31 presenting 77.5 percent have between 1 and 4 adult relatives who depend on them for some or most of their needs. A lower percentage of 7.5 percent indicated having more that 5 adult relatives that they support. However, 6 respondents representing 15 percent of the sample had no adult dependents.

Table 7.5 Adult dependents

Number of	Frequency	Percent

dependents		
No dependents	6	15.0
1-4	31	77.5
5+	3	7.5
Total operators	40	100

These figures underscore the social as well as economic significance of informality in the livelihood strategy of bicycle taxi and handcart or wheelbarrow operators and numerous people connected with them, including their spouses and children, parents and relatives living in rural villages, and other relations and kin in and outside the city. Evidently, the informal economy helps keep social support systems and the extended family system alive and it is one of the conduits through which rural-urban interconnections can be appreciated.

These observations reflect the high dependency ratio and the extended family system prevalent in Malawi. Extended family systems are characteristic of most African societies. Lourenco-Lindell (2002) showed that kinship based ties are amplified as the basis for social networking in many West African cities. A study of the informal economy in the capital of Guinea Bissau revealed a situation whereby informal work was structured around the extended family system and there were many instances of interdependence between multi-spatial household units (Lourenco-Lindell, 2002).

Educational attainment levels of the bicycle taxi and handcart operators

The majority of the bicycle taxi and handcart or wheelbarrow operators have very little education to get formal employment or to enter formal training institutions (Figure 7.4). Out of the 40 respondents, only 4 had the Malawi School Certificate of Education (MSCE), which is the secondary or high school diploma, representing 10 percent of the sample, while 10 had a Junior Certificate of Education (JCE), or junior high school diploma, representing 25 percent. The majority left school after passing the Primary School Leaving Certificate (PSLC) examination. These formed 60 percent of the sample. Two more respondents left school during primary classes. These findings agree with my previous survey conducted in 2002 on street vending in Blantyre where out of a sample of 100 street vendors, 4 percent had no formal schooling, 6 percent had the MSCE, 18 percent the JCE and

72 percent left school at different stages in primary school (Jimu, 2003).

Figure 7.4 Levels of educational attainment

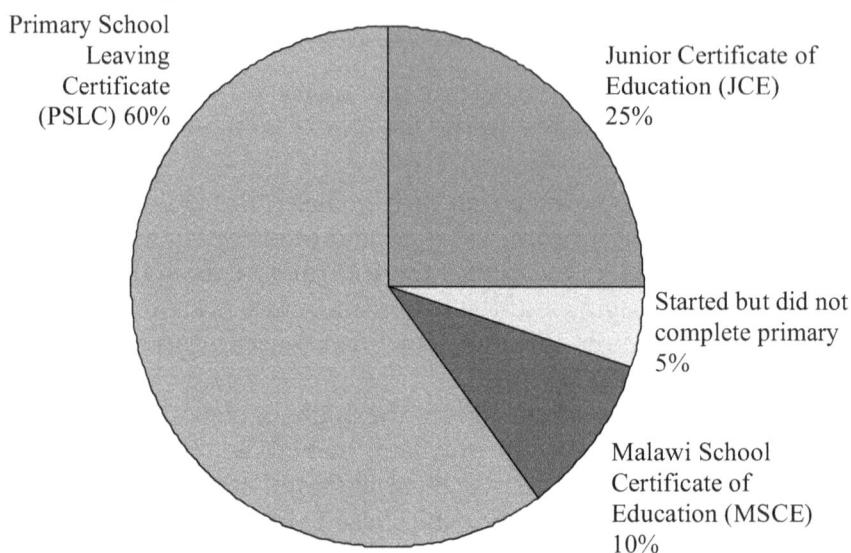

Primary School Leaving Certificate (PSLC) 60%

Junior Certificate of Education (JCE) 25%

Started but did not complete primary 5%

Malawi School Certificate of Education (MSCE) 10%

It is not evident on the basis of current data whether lack of or little formal education is the main factor driving people into these occupations, though nothing is unique about this scenario which seems to be a norm among informal economy workers. Apparently, out of the 21 bicycle taxi operators surveyed, only 9 had attended secondary school education representing about 43 percent compared to 5 out of 19 handcart operators which represents about 26 percent. However, there were more handcart operators than bicycle taxi operators who attended and completed primary schooling but did not proceed to secondary school. Of the 19 handcart operators surveyed 13 representing 68 percent completed primary school compared to 11 out of 21 bicycle taxi operators, representing 52 percent. These statistics are significant in a number of ways. First, these activities are for people with low educational attainment levels, though some people with moderate levels are also involved, largely because of the problem of high unemployment rates dealt with in the next chapter. Second, these statistics confirm observations in other studies conducted within and outside Africa. For instance, in South Africa 95 percent of all informal economy workers had not completed high school as of 2003. In El Salvador in Central America, as of 2002, 21 percent of all informal workers had no formal schooling or education. It appears that where formal education does not guarantee formal employment, there is no incentive for the underprivileged to strive for better education. Highly educated people end up working in the informal economy. For example, the same report noted that 5 percent of workers in Egypt's informal economy had a university or post graduate degree (Economic Policy Institute/Global Policy Network, Undated).

Dynamics of residence in Mzuzu

All the bicycle taxi and handcart operators involved in the study reported living in Mzuzu for varying lengths of time and in different locations, however, they all indicated living in locations designated as traditional high density areas.

Duration of residence in Mzuzu

The duration of residence in Mzuzu has little effect on the decision to engage in the informal economy as bicycle taxi or handcart operator. The respondents to this survey had lived in Mzuzu city for periods ranging from a few months to more than 10 years (Table 7.6). Some of the operators have lived in Mzuzu since birth.

Table 7.6 Duration of residence in Mzuzu

Duration	Frequency	Percent
< 1 year	5	12.5
1-5 years	13	32.5
6-10 years	8	20
> 10 years	14	35.0
Total respondents	40	100

Over half of the bicycle taxi and handcart operators have lived in Mzuzu for more than five years. Out of the 40 respondents, 14 have been living in Mzuzu for over 10 years. This represents 35 percent of the sample. In terms of significance, this is followed by those who have lived in Mzuzu city for periods ranging from one to five years, then six to ten years and finally the least significant is the category of those who have lived in Mzuzu for periods ranging from a few months to one year. These figures indicate that by and large most of the bicycle and handcart operators arrived in Mzuzu after the reintroduction of multiparty politics and the adoption of accelerated economic liberalisation policies in the mid 1990s. In my earlier survey of street vending in Blantyre in 2002-3, I noted that these two factors are very significant in understanding the growth, dynamics and politics of the informal economy. In many ways they played a catalytic role, as discussed in chapter 5.

Characteristics of places of residence

The urban poor, who are unable to compete for scarce resources or protect themselves from harmful environmental conditions, are most affected by the negative impacts of urbanisation. The growth of cities has been accompanied by an increase in urban poverty which tends to be concentrated in certain social groups and in particular locations. In case of bicycle taxi and handcart operators, it was observed that they all live in high density traditional (HDT) housing estates (Table 7.7). These are residential areas that have developed without the benefit of prior planning and often on fragile environments such as natural drainage waterways and flood-prone areas. They are characterized by inadequate housing and poor provision of infrastructure such as roads, street lights, water, sanitation and waste management services.

Table 7.7 Residential areas

Residential area	Frequency	Percent	Valid percent	Cumulative percent
Area 1B	1	2.5	2.5	2.5
Chibavi	3	7.5	7.5	10.0
Ching'ambo	2	5.0	5.0	15.0
Chiputula	6	15.0	15.0	30.0
Luwinga	1	2.5	2.5	32.5
Masasa	5	12.5	12.5	45.0
Mchengautuwa	16	40.0	40.0	85.0
Mphaka	1	2.5	2.5	87.5
Sonda	1	2.5	2.5	90.0
Sozibele	1	2.5	2.5	92.5
Zolozolo	3	7.5	7.5	100
Total operators	40	100	100	

Most of the buildings or dwelling units are constructed using simple materials. For example, houses are constructed of green (unburnt) bricks and mud mortar, and the roofing is made of either grass thatch or iron sheets. Out of the 40 respondents, 31 were hesitant to comment on the nature of the houses where they live. However, the 9 respondents that came forward with information on this aspect revealed that a majority of the bicycle taxi and handcart operators live in grass thatched houses. Out of the 9 respondents, 7 live in grass thatched houses as opposed to 2 who indicated living in houses with iron sheet roofing. Grass thatched houses, except those with plastic sheets, often leak when it rains and are a fire hazard. Grass thatched houses are a norm in rural areas and a symbol of permanence but in urban areas they signify poverty and to a great degree impermanence. Over time, grass thatched houses are replaced by iron sheet roofed houses. The occupants are eventually displaced because improvement comes along with hikes in monthly rentals and if the current occupants cannot afford revised rentals they are pushed to even poorer areas farther away from the city centre. High density traditional areas experience numerous problems related to service provision. For example, there are often problems of access to running water, electricity and sanitation. Some areas are located in water logged parts of Mzuzu city. Examples include Chiputula, Ching'ambo, Chibavi, and Sozibele residential areas. These areas are infested with mosquitoes and thus prone to malaria.

Photo 7.1 Aerial overview of Sozibele and Chibavi townships

Photo 7.2 Children playing outside grass thatched house in Sozibele

Photo 7.3 Grass thatched house built using green bricks, plastered and painted white in a waterlogged environment. Sugarcane appearing in front favours high water areas.

Photo 7.4 Grass thatched house adjacent to iron sheet roofed house. Electric power lines pass above the grass thatched house.

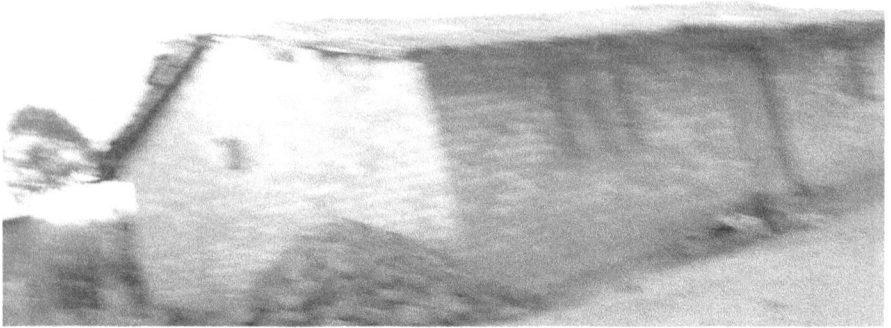

Photo 7.5 Grass thatched house built using fire cured bricks. Grass thatch will soon be replaced by iron sheets and the house will be connected to electricity (see the meter box on the western wall). A hike in rental will force current occupants to relocate.

Most of the bicycle taxi and handcart operators seem to live in rented houses. Twenty one respondents were hesitant to comment on whether they live in their own houses or in rented houses. However, out of the 19 that responded to this question, 18 live in rented houses and only 1 lives in his own house (Table 7.8).

Table 7.8 Home ownership

Status	Frequency	Percent
Hesitant to respond	21	52.5
Rented	18	45.0
Self owned	1	2.5
Total respondents	40	100

This partly reflects the fact that 65% of the bicycle taxi and handcart operators have been in Mzuzu for only ten or fewer years and are therefore not yet established. It also reflects the position of most bicycle taxi and handcart operators in the socio-economic hierarchy of Mzuzu city. Bicycle taxi and handcart operators live in high density traditional areas, and in such areas house rental is relatively low (Table 7.9). The opportunity costs of acquiring a plot and building a house are higher than the opportunity costs of renting. This may as well be a reflection of the prohibitive costs of building materials.

Table 7.9 Monthly house rentals

Monthly house rental (MWK)	Frequency	Percent
300	4	10.0
500	3	7.5
550	1	2.5
700	1	2.5
800	1	2.5
900	1	2.5
Total responses	11	27.5
No response	29	72.5
Total operators	40	100.0

It was observed that monthly rentals range from K300 to K900. Out of the 11 respondents, 4 representing 36.4 percent live in houses attracting a monthly rental of K300.00. Three respondents live in houses whose monthly rental is K500.00. This represents 27.3 percent of the respondents to this question. The remaining 4 respondents live in houses attracting monthly rentals of K550.00, K700.00, K800.00 and K900.00. In general terms, the monthly rentals are very low reflecting the low quality of structures and the socio-economic status of the tenants.

Photo 7.6 Public water kiosk in Chibavi township

Conclusion

Given the observations above, it is clear that people involved in the informal economy as bicycle taxi and handcart operators fall within the low socio-economic status. This is evident from their social characteristics, in particular levels of educational attainment, places of residence and accessibility to social services in their areas of residence. In terms of educational attainment, the majority of bicycle taxi and handcart operators are semi-literate. Well over half of the sampled population has not attained post primary education. Hence, most of the operators do not have employable skills acquired through formal training. All bicycle taxi and handcart operators live in high density traditional areas or slums that are poorly serviced. Most of them live in houses that are temporary to semi permanent in nature. Although the Mzuzu city assembly has been upgrading the traditional high density residential areas by constructing access roads and with the support of the Northern Region Water Board extended piped water to these residential areas, the conditions are far from satisfactory. These are challenges of urban development in Malawi. At the root of urban poverty lies the shortage of jobs and of opportunities to earn an income through decent work. Urban development policies should vigorously address the issue of livelihoods together with the improvement of housing, infrastructure, and environmental conditions. The next chapter focuses on the economic situation of bicycle taxi and handcart operators. It attempts to explain how the social attributes described in this chapter and the context described in earlier chapters have facilitated and nurtured the proliferation of bicycle taxi and handcart operations.

Chapter Eight

ECONOMIC PROFILE OF THE OPERATORS

This chapter provides an overview of economic factors that lead to informality in the urban transport sector from the perspective of the operators. In other words, the focus is on the economic profile of the operators. Lack of meaningful employment opportunities and poverty characterise informal sector workers and explain the proliferation of the informal economy. Although the survey leading to this publication did not succeed at gathering substantive data on average incomes nor on other quantifiable dimensions of the economic life of bicycle taxi and handcart or wheelbarrow operators, qualitative assessments and other indirect measures show that their activities make a significant contribution to the economic life of the operators and their families. The argument advanced in this chapter is that the significance of bicycle taxi and handcart operators can be appreciated by paying attention to proxy indices of income earned and redistributed through the various ways the operators dispose of their incomes, qualitative linkages with other economic and social activities, and above all the advantages outlined by the operators themselves.

Employment and unemployment

It appears that bicycle taxi and handcart operations are choices of last resort. That is, most people join only when they have failed elsewhere. As we saw in Table 7.2 in the previous chapter, 28 participants representing 70 percent of the sample migrated to Mzuzu to seek formal employment and only one representing 2.5 percent came to Mzuzu with the sole intention of operating a bicycle taxi business.

Considering the various motivations, it is evident that bicycle taxi and handcart or wheelbarrow activities are important sources of employment, self employment in particular. Out of the 40 bicycle taxi and handcart operators involved in the study, 36 representing 90 percent were self employed. At least 32 representing 80 percent indicated owning the bicycles and handcarts they used, while 4 operators representing 10 percent use hired bicycles or wheelbarrows. The remaining 4 respondents representing another 10 percent used a bicycle or wheelbarrow belonging to a brother or other close relative (Table 8.1). This shows the importance of kinship in the informal transport sector.

Table 8.1 Ownership of bicycles and handcarts (wheelbarrows)

Owner	Frequency	Percent
Brother	1	2.5
Other close	3	7.5
relative	4	10.0
Hired	32	80.0
Owned by	40	100
operator		
Total operators		

Sources of money used to purchase bicycles and handcarts

It appears that there are different sources of financing or capital used to purchase bicycles and handcarts in Mzuzu city (Table 8.2).

Table 8.2 Sources of money used to purchase bicycles or handcarts in use

Source of money	Frequency	Percent
Hired bicycle/handcart	4	10.0
Gift from parents	2	5.0
Savings from business	10	25.0
Savings from employment	14	35.0
Savings from farming (rural)	2	5.0
Savings from hired bicycle	1	2.5
Savings from hired handcart	6	15.0
Savings from informal	1	2.5
economy	40	100
Total operators		

Savings from previous employment and business appear to be the dominant sources of income used to purchase the bicycles and handcarts. Out of the 40 respondents, 14 representing 35 percent, and 10 representing 25 percent purchased bicycles and handcarts using savings from previous employment and businesses, respectively. The next most important sources of capital are savings from hired handcarts, savings from farming and gifts from parents. Only 4 operators representing 10 percent, as indicated in this Table and in Table 8.1, used hired bicycles or handcarts at the time of the survey.

Length of involvement in bicycle taxi and handcart business

Transport via bicycle taxi and handcart is well established though these operations have not been in practice for a long period of time. Most of the respondents have been involved in these activities for less than 5 years. In fact, 12 of the respondents representing 30 percent of the total sample size had been involved in these activities for less than half a year at the time of the survey. Another 10 representing 25 percent had been in these activities for about a year, while 1 representing 2.5 percent had been involved for periods extending to 1.5, 2 and 8 years each. Only one respondent had been involved for more than 10 years.

Two points ought to be noted from these observations. First, bicycle taxis have been in operation for just over 2 years whereas handcarts have been in use for more. Hence, while all the bicycle operators are newcomers, some handcart operators have been in business for a long period of time. Two of the participants reported operating handcarts for 8 and 14 years each. The second observation is that these activities are refugee occupations. As such, there are new entrants and exits at any time, and few operators persist. This observation does not however imply that these operations are transitory in nature; rather the operators join and exit as fast as they can. The intention for the majority is to get as much money as possible in the shortest possible period of time to venture into other business or occupations.

Motives for engaging in bicycle taxi and handcart business

The majority of the bicycle taxi and handcart operators turned to these occupations after they migrated to Mzuzu and failed to secure employment. These activities appear thus to be survival strategies for groups of people who have been relegated to work and eke out a meagre existence in 'the dungeons of the informal sector' (Rogerson and Hart, 1989: 29). They represent one particular avenue of 'legitimation and recognition' for recent migrants who find the 'promises of modernity are fast becoming a broken dream for all but an elite few' (Nyamnjoh, 2002: 118, 120).

However, different operators sited different and varied reasons for joining these occupations (Figure 8.1).

Figure 8.1 Reasons for joining bicycle taxi and handcart operations

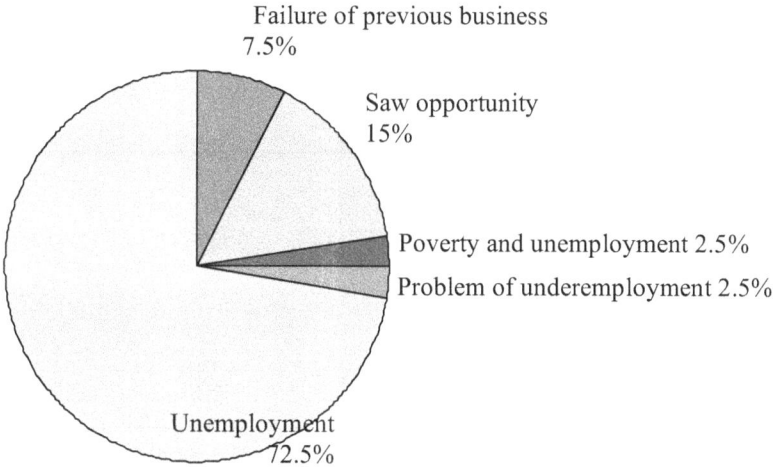

Failure of previous business
7.5%

Saw opportunity
15%

Poverty and unemployment 2.5%

Problem of underemployment 2.5%

Unemployment
72.5%

It was noted that out of the sample size of 40, a total of 29 respondents, representing 72.5 percent, described their entry into these two occupations as a response to failure to get a job that could enable them on a sustainable basis to access the basic needs of food, clothing and shelter. Other motivations were underemployment (2.5 percent), poverty and unemployment (2.5 percent), failure of previous business (7.5 percent) and opportunity to increase income (15 percent). These motivations suggest that bicycle taxi and handcart operators are not a homogeneous group. In fact they can be differentiated according to their motivations as well as aspirations. Although many operators joined because they were despondent, some joined because they perceived opportunities to improve per capita income levels and advance in life. These are success seekers, most of whom have alternative income earning activities. Such operators are involved in straddling (see Chapter 9).

Real incomes

As compared to my study of street vending in Blantyre in 2002-3 and other similar studies in other countries, bicycle taxi and handcart operators earn invariably higher incomes. It was noted that daily incomes sometimes approach K 1 000.00. While most of the participants indicated that daily earnings range from K 500.00 to K 750.00, only one participant ever experienced a daily income higher than K 1 000.00 (Table 8.3).

Table 8.3 Average incomes per day

Average daily income (MWK)	Frequency	Percent
200	1	2.5
500	26	65.0
750	12	30.0
1 000	1	2.5
Total operators	40	100.0

In the survey, the income amounts in Table 8.3 were not premeditated but rather approximated at the time of data analysis. To minimize categories, all incomes above K 200.00 were rounded to the nearest K 250.00. This also reflects the inexactness with which participants expressed their incomes. Most gave higher income figures at first and later adjusted the estimations downwards when data collectors came up with follow up questions. This is an indication that the operators were uncertain about their daily incomes or not keen to disclose exact amounts. This is common among informal businesspeople. Income is also quite often under reported to evade paying tax or discourage prospective entrants, thereby minimizing competition.

It appears that daily income for bicycle and handcart operators is nonetheless higher than for other local occupations, and well above the government minimum wage of K 86.00 per day in urban areas. This explains the involvement of people with junior and senior secondary certificates as well as those employed in other occupations, for example as shop assistants, plumbers and security guards. It should also be noted that bicycle taxi operators reported higher levels of income as compared to handcart operators. Current data sets do not offer clues to the possible explanation for this occurrence. I can however surmise that the bicycle taxi operators serve far more clients in a day covering longer and more varied distances than the handcart operators. These factors are reflected in higher rates from clients.

Perceptions of and satisfaction with income levels from respective activities

Although most of the bicycle taxi and handcart operators could be described as opportunists by the mere fact that their activities flourish due to the constraints created by undeveloped motorized transport systems and therefore unresolved problems of mobility, few are comfortable with their daily incomes. Out of the 40 respondents, 19 representing 47.5 percent reported that the level of daily income has been declining while 7 representing 17.5 percent reported incomes growing steadily since they joined. The remaining 14 respondents reported that incomes have been stagnant (27.5 percent) or unstable (7.5 percent) (Figure 8.2). There is no clearly defined connection or relationship between length of time in the occupation and the level of income over time, despite that rising competition owing to an increase in the number of people joining in the occupation has the effect of depressed income levels.

Figure 8.2 Perceptions of levels of income

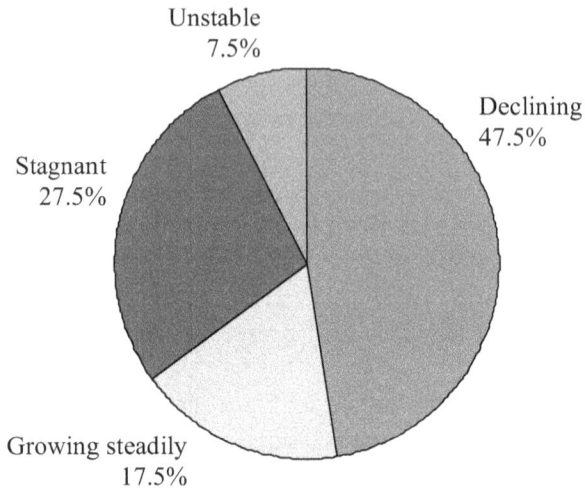

While17.5 percent of the respondents seemed comfortable with the prevailing levels of income, when asked whether or not they were satisfied with their current income levels, 14 operators representing 35 percent reported that they are satisfied while 26 representing a whooping 65 percent reported lack of satisfaction (Figure 8.3).

Figure 8.3 Satisfaction with current levels of income

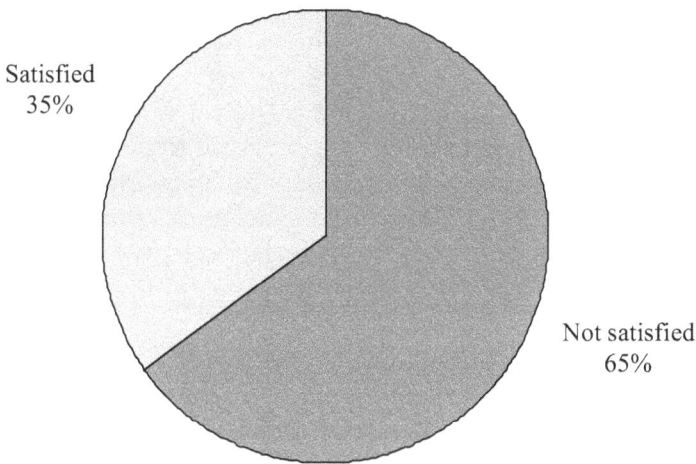

Satisfied
35%

Not satisfied
65%

There was notable variation in the reasons for lack of satisfaction (Table 8.4). Those not satisfied are greater in number, yet some experiencing a decline in income or unstable income flows were satisfied with whatever little they get by the end of the day. This is an indication of the fact that no matter how small the daily income may be, it is better than none and possibly because of the observation made earlier about incomes being on the higher side when compared with other informal economy occupations. The picture becomes more nuanced however when we factor in intentions to quit. It appeared that most of the bicycle taxi and handcart operators had plans or were willing to quit these occupations at some point in the future.

Table 8.4 Reasons for being satisfied or not satisfied

Satisfied	Not satisfied
• The money I get enables me to buy food and other supplies for my family (bi & cart). • It satisfies my basic needs. • It depends on how business is going on. • Am able to satisfy my needs and other dependants' needs (bi & cart).	• Money not adequate to address my needs (bi & cart). • Instability of income (bi & cart). • The income is not enough to make a substantial savings to buffer insecurity of income when the bicycle or cart has broken down.

• It is an alternative and extra source of income to my work as plumber. • At least it is enough to buy food on a daily basis (wheelbarrow operator). • At first I was doing nothing (wheelbarrow operator).	• My target is K 1 000.00 but I fail to reach that figure. • More problems faced at home than money realized in a day (bi & cart). • Income is very small as compared to number of dependents (cart). • Income is small and it has to be shared between myself and the owner of the wheelbarrow.

I noted that out of the 40 respondents, 28 representing 70 percent have plans or are willing to quit and do something different. This leaves 12 respondents representing 30 percent neither planning nor willing to consider quitting at the moment (Figure 8.4).

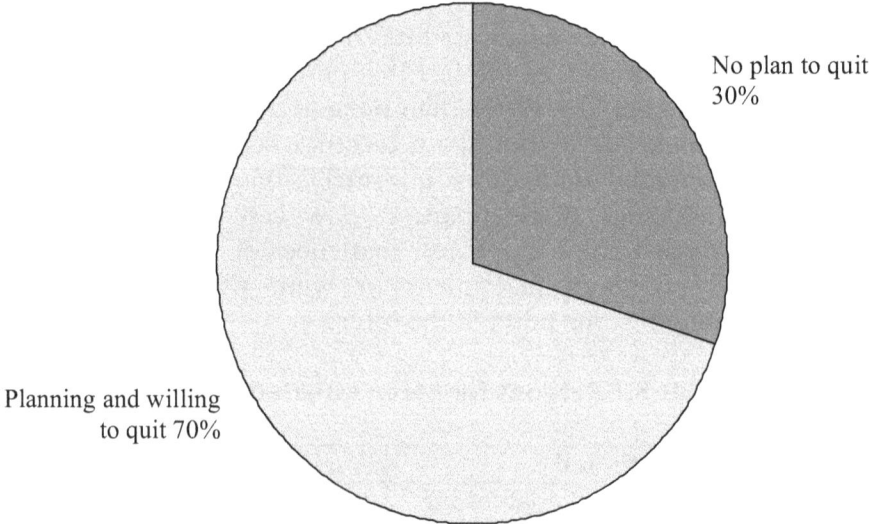

No plan to quit 30%

Planning and willing to quit 70%

Figure 8.4 Plans and willingness to quit

The reasons given for plans or willingness to quit ranged from personal misgivings, existence of opportunities elsewhere, constraints encountered in the course of these occupations or other occupations in other localities, energy demands required for these occupations as well as availability or lack thereof of outside support. Some of the specific reasons mentioned by the operators that have plans or are willing to quit included:

- To start a business because income from bicycle taxi and handcart activities is not adequate to meet all needs. Sometimes the income is not high enough to sustain a meaningful life in the city;
- To go home (rural village) and try other activities;
- To find a better job or any chance to do something different and profitable;
- One who trained as a carpenter plans to quit as soon as he has manages to save enough money to buy tools for a carpentry shop;
- Two operators, one a bicycle taxi and the other a handcart operator, are planning to migrate to South Africa as soon as they raise enough money for the bus fare and other immediate ancillary expenses;
- One bicycle taxi operator described his work as a hard way of earning a living that does not tally with his academic qualifications. Apparently, he has a Malawi School Certificate of Education (MSCE) which is a basic qualification for most training institutions and jobs in both the private and public sectors.

On the other hand, those who have no plans and are unwilling to quit these occupations derive satisfaction from the work, in which their income earning ability has improved, or they have no options other than the current occupations. They joined because they perceived an opportunity or are desperate for alternative occupations. Some of the specific issues mentioned in the survey by operators in this category are:

- These activities represent one of the avenues for better income earning opportunities. For example, one bicycle taxi operator reported incomes from these operations to be higher than what he gets from working with one of the big construction companies in Malawi;
- Bicycle taxis and handcarts are the only viable sources of self-employment;
- Some operators meet their daily needs through these activities, although the income may not be adequate or enough all the time;
- Pessimism that the high unemployment rate and current joblessness could be overcome.

Straddling the formal/informal divide

Although the majority of the bicycle taxi and handcart operators rely solely on incomes from one of the two occupations, some have additional or alternative sources of income (Figure 8.5). This means that variation and diversity or straddling characterize some bicycle taxi and handcart operators' livelihoods. Englund (2002) argued that central to this imagery of straddling is the combination of livelihood strategies in different places and with different partners. Out of the 40 respondents, 28 representing 70 percent of the sample had no alternative sources of income besides bicycle taxi and handcart operations. This means that only 12 participants representing 30 percent of the respondents had other sources of income.

Figure 8.5 Alternative sources of income

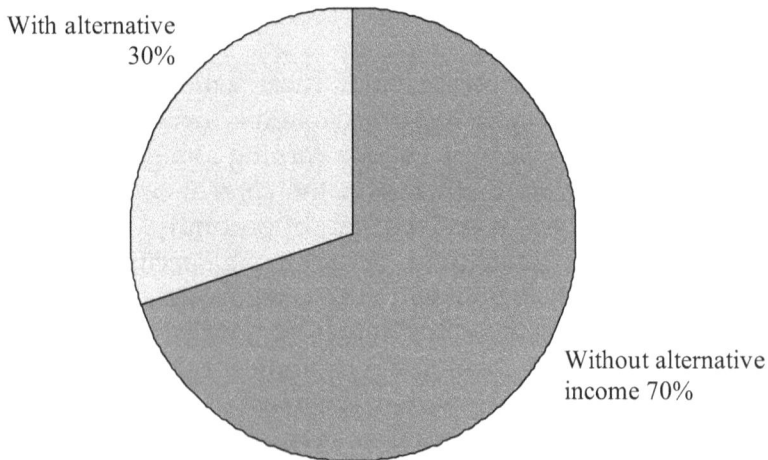

With alternative 30%

Without alternative income 70%

Although the majority of the operators do not have alternative sources of income, it does not follow that these two occupations are the only openings available for the people involved nor that the informal economy is the only means by which poor people can earn a living. However, considering the dismal development of the private sector in Mzuzu city, poor educational attainment by most of the bicycle taxi and handcart operators, and the general decline in economic activities in Malawi as a whole over the last decade and a half, the informal economy remains the main and potentially viable option in the foreseeable future. No wonder that most of the alternative sources of income are informal in nature. The operators that indicated having alternative sources of income were involved in one of the following ten occupations:

- Two respondents work as security guards at the homes of the middle class in Mapale residential estate;
- One bicycle taxi operator is a part-time electrician. He learned the trade on the job and he does not have any formal training and certification;
- One bicycle taxi operator has a bicycle repair workshop;
- One bicycle taxi operator is employed by G4S Securicor (Malawi), an international security company;
- One bicycle taxi operator is a part-time carpenter;
- One bicycle taxi operator is a plumber and he works with SR Nicholas construction company;
- One wheelbarrow operator also works as a bus loader in the depot;
- One wheelbarrow operator is a bricklayer but he does not have tools. He acquired the skill on the job;
- One wheelbarrow operator is involved in rice cultivation in Karonga;
- One more wheelbarrow operator runs a butchery where he sells goat meat and pork.

Of the 12 that indicated having alternative sources of income, 9 happened to be bicycle taxi operators, representing 75 percent of the sample having alternative income sources, and 22.5 percent of the total sample population. Of all bicycle taxi operators in the sample, 43% have alternative income sources while only 16% of the handcart operators do. This suggests that bicycle taxi operators exploit other opportunities in the formal and informal sectors more so than do handcart operators. Yet, bicycle taxi owners are also more mobile and the number of operators as well as the amount of daily income is on the higher side. This observation conveys a sense of creativity and voluntarism among the bicycle taxi operators.

I noted a similar evidence of straddling in 2002 while studying the growth, dynamics and politics of street vending in Blantyre. Apart from making sales in the streets, the vendors pursued other income-earning opportunities on and off the streets. I also noted that although these extra income opportunities were not regular, they meant a lot to the street vendors by augmenting what appeared to be highly erratic (Jimu, 2003). Straddling or the alternative opportunities per se cannot be ignored, in a context of desperate experimentation under abject economic conditions.

Patronage of bicycle taxis and handcarts

The services offered by bicycle taxi and handcart operators attract more clients. Most bicycle and handcart operators reported serving at least 15 to 20 clients a day. The main clients are businesspeople. A sizable proportion of the clients are involved in other informal economy occupations such as street and market vending, retailing, timber retailing and construction (Figure 8.6).

Figure 8.6 Occupations of main clients

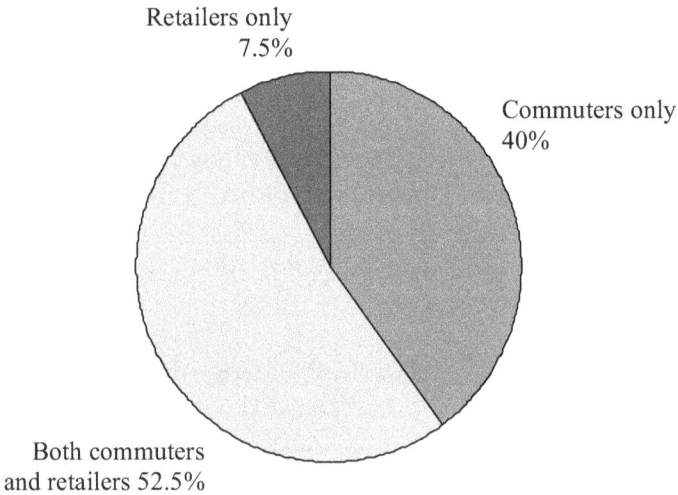

Retailers only
7.5%

Commuters only
40%

Both commuters
and retailers 52.5%

The beneficiaries are both male and female. As pointed out in the previous chapter, out of the 40 respondents, 17 representing 42.5 percent reported having an equal number of male and female clients. However, 15 representing 37.5 percent reported that most of the clients were male, while 8 representing 20 percent reported that females constituted the majority of the clients.

Photo 8.1 Bicycle taxi operator carrying a female client along Chibavi road

Photo 8.2 Three children on one bicycle taxi carrier to school

It is clear that these occupations respond to the social and economic needs of both male and female clients (Figure 8.7).

Figure 8.7 Gender of most clients

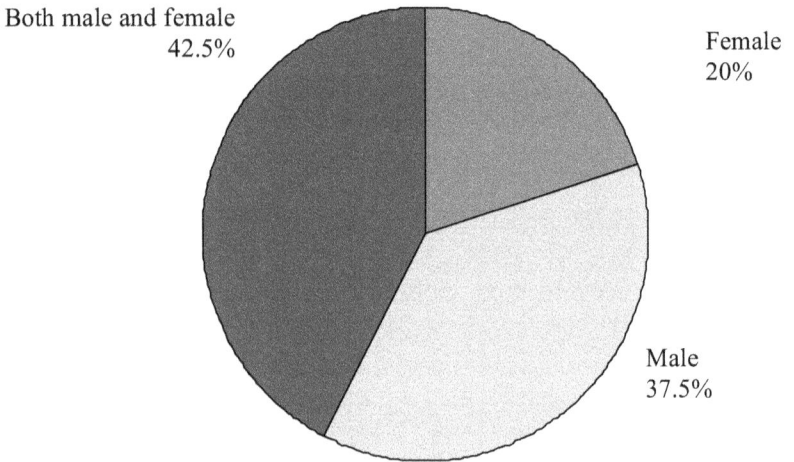

Both male and female
42.5%

Female
20%

Male
37.5%

Apparently bicycle taxi and handcart or wheelbarrow services are affordable and readily available. These forms of transport provide linkages between localities within the city as well as nearby villages and market centres located at the outskirt of Mzuzu city and some locations several kilometres away from Mzuzu. Wheelbarrow operators support the informal economy, as depicted in Photo 8.3.

Photo 8.3 A bag of second-hand clothes in a wheelbarrow to the market

Conclusion

The benefits of the informal economy are most often underrepresented despite its contributions to the livelihood strategies of people, most of whom are poor. Lack of recordkeeping skills and limited awareness of the importance of the same makes it almost impossible to obtain accurate information on average incomes from informal workers. The scenario is compounded by the mistrust that informal workers feel towards outsiders seeking in depth information on the performance of business in the informal sector. Fearful of the long hand of government regulation, tax and licensing regimes in particular, informal economy workers quite often disguise and misrepresent their incomes to escape taxation.

This chapter has demonstrated the productivity of business in the informal sector and its significance by focusing on indicators other than just income. These include, but are not limited to, the place of informal economy activities in the livelihood and income strategies of bicycle and handcart operators, degree of satisfaction with the levels of income, plans and willingness to quit as well as involvement in and motives for alternative income earning activities. Considering all these questions requires in depth studies other than quantitative questionnaire based research approaches and is imperative to ascertain and substantiate the role of the informal economy in the development process.

With respect to the economic dynamics of bicycle taxi and handcart operators as presented in this chapter, it is apparent that the informal economy continues to grow in inverse proportion to the decline of the formal economy and that its activities respond to societal needs for mobility and livelihood. There is a great deal of flexibility, adaptive-ness and innovation that the formal economy cannot replicate. As has been shown in this chapter and is developed further in the next, these activities contribute to the economy of Mzuzu city through employment creation and income distribution. Somehow they have multiplier effects through the hierarchical and lateral linkages within the informal economy and with other sector. I noted with keen interest the flourishing of roadside bicycle repair workshops that serve mainly the bicycle taxi operators. It is evident that these activities are important though at the moment it is difficult to quantify the contribution they make to general economic welfare in the city. Although people may be poor and not have cash or savings, they do have and harness other assets like kinship, time and zeal, as evidenced by the diverse ways in which bicycle and handcart operators manage economic life despite the odds of unemployment and other challenges of urbanisation. The next chapter provides a qualitative appraisal of the economic as well as social value of the informal economy and challenges that operators encounter.

Chapter Nine

APPROPRIATING URBANISATION THROUGH SOCIO-ECONOMIC INFORMALITY

The purpose of this chapter is to integrate the socio-economic profiles of bicycle taxi and handcart operators with the urbanisation framework provided in the initial chapters. The operationalisation of linkage between urbanisation and informality in the first five chapters emphasizes the significance of rural-urban migration and demographic change as well as economic and political liberalisation in the 1990s. In a modicum way, this chapter contributes to the debate on the dynamics of connections between urban informal businesses and the formal sector. While acknowledging and drawing from my previous contributions on the subject and those of other scholars, this chapter attempts specifically to relate the socio-economic profile of informal economy workers to growing unemployment, hopelessness and economic insecurity experienced by the marginally employed. In other words, emphasis is on the real politics of the informal economy in Mzuzu city.

Writing about *Informal Politics* in Mexico City, Cross (1998) suggested the need to understand the specifics and the context circumscribing the informal economy in a particular situation. The context of this study has been articulated specifically in chapter three, and more generally in chapters four and five. Pryor's (1990: 12) distinction of 'old' political economy, which focuses on the role of historical, cultural and ideological factors, and the 'new' political economy, which focuses on the interactions of interest groups in maximizing self interests (Jimu, 2003), is useful for understanding the socio-economic profiles and popularity of bicycle taxi and handcart or wheelbarrow operations in Mzuzu city. Disaggregating the 'old' and 'new' political economy is a challenge that this chapter has in a modicum way met by focusing on the interactions of interest groups in maximizing self interests, in other words by zooming in on scenes of the lived in universe of the operators. The experiences, motivations and aspirations of informal economy workers expressed in their life stories show that economic informality in towns and cities reflects and in some cases represents new frontiers and battle lines against poverty, unemployment and underemployment as well as social inequalities that come with rapid urbanisation. These perspectives come from an appreciation of informality as a way of life, along with an understanding of the spatial significance of bicycle taxi and handcart operations.

Informality as a way of life

Laguerre (1994: 32) in *The Informal City* noted that informality is characterized by the intentionality or personal needs of the actor with the individual often aware of his or her unconventional action. What makes the informal economy unconventional is that most activities are *not registered* or licensed and *unregulated* and quite often largely subsistence in orientation, involving the poor who tend to be self-employed (Republic of Malawi, 2000c). The root causes of the growth of the informal economy are unemployment, growing urban poverty and precarious socio-economic opportunities, which tend to preclude a growing proportion of urban populations from enjoying promises of success associated with living in cities and towns (Hart, 1973; Hope, 1997, 2001; Post 1996). This scenario is often explained as the aftermath of rapid urbanisation, the product of high birth and rural-urban migration rates. Over time, and as many more people are born in or migrate to cities and towns, the rate of increase in the size of urban populations exceeds by far the rate of increase in meaningful employment opportunities (Hope, 1997: 30).

The division of economic activities into discreet spheres such as formal and informal, official and unofficial, or regular and irregular economies (Hope, 2001) is important for both analytical and empirical purposes. The bicycle taxi and handcart operators in this study are empirical representation of the informal economy. As highlighted in the initial chapter, the worldwide growth of the 'informal' economy is often symptomatic of growing unemployment, poor working conditions such as low income levels, poor labour standards and the inability of most workers to move up in the labour markets. There is growing understanding, despite the assumption that there are different economic sectors, that informal economy workers do not operate a distinct economy but rather have been pushed to the edges of the formal economy (War on Want et al., 2006). This is well illustrated by the socio-economic attributes of bicycle taxi and handcart or wheelbarrow operators, discussed in chapters seven and eight. From their life stories presented in this chapter, it is apparent that most people working in the informal economy can hardly find formal employment and that any job appears better than none. Together with street and market vendors, bicycle, radio and shoe repairers, and small workshop owners and their employees, and workers such as bicycle taxi and handcart operators form the lower circuitry of the economy of Mzuzu city, as in the economies of other cities in the developing world (Santos, 1979). These dimensions are reflected in the life stories of Fuke and Jere.

Life story of Fuke

Fuke started in the bicycle taxi business sometime back in Karonga Township, 200 km north of Mzuzu, where bicycle taxis are known as 'cargo'. He dropped out of school in standard six. He came to Mzuzu in June 2005 to run a bicycle taxi. He brought the bicycle he was using at the time of the survey from Karonga. He bought it after saving wages from piecework (*ganyu*). He came to Mzuzu after hearing that the bicycle taxi operators in Mzuzu earn a more descent income than those in Karonga. He lives alone in Chibavi Township in a rented house. His monthly rental is K300.00. He is single. On good days he earns about K800.00. He uses the income to support himself, as well as his parents in Karonga. His short term plan is to buy a second bicycle, which he can hire out to other would be operators. In this way, he will diversify income sources within the bicycle taxi business. His main challenge is instability of income, largely due to competition among the bicycle taxi operators. Although the daily income is unstable, he does not have plans to quit or return to Karonga. He was optimistic that the business environment will improve within two months during the season when farmers sell agricultural produce.

Fuke's story is not unique as there are many in his situation. The story of Sata shared in chapter 6 is similar as is that of a bicycle taxi operator only known as Jere.

Life story of Jere

Jere was one of the first people who joined the bicycle taxi business in early 2004. He is a bona fide bicycle taxi operator with an ID issued by the Mzuzu Bicycle Operators Association. He described his entry as out of necessity. He failed to continue his education, due to lack of financial support, after passing his JCE. Although he was offered support by a cousin, he was badly treated and the conditions at his cousin's home were not conducive to schooling. For a short period of time he worked as a house servant in Lilongwe. He left the job after suffering an injury on the job. He used the money he received as compensation to start a small business, but he could hardly survive on proceeds from the business. He bought a second hand bicycle which he uses as a taxi. He went on to buy another second hand bicycle. Later he bought a new bicycle. He is hiring out two of the three bicycles. He receives a commission of K200 per day from the operators. Since joining the bicycle taxi business, in addition to owning three bicycles, he bought a piece of land in one of the high density traditional areas (Mchengautuwa) where he has erected a house in which he is living at the moment. He is now married. He used income from the bicycle taxi business to settle the bride wealth (*lobola*).

Kondwani, a wheelbarrow operator from Mzimba district, also has a similar story. His destitution, marginal employment and misfortunes of childlessness are linked, though the connections are not as obvious as for the others.

Life story of Kondwani

Kondwani was born in Mpherembe in 1973. He went to school from 1980 to 1987 and dropped in standard seven. He worked as a houseboy for a year. He later went to Embangweni where he lived with his grandmother for some two years between 1992 and 1994. In 1994 he got married and went back to Mpherembe. He came to Mzuzu in 1999 to look for work. Between 2000 and 2002 he worked as a watchman. In 2002 he bought a wheelbarrow and has since lived on the proceeds from operating it. He lives in Masasa, one of the high density traditional housing areas a kilometre and a half from Mzuzu central business district. He had a lame child who later died after Kondwani sought medication for the child from several hospitals.

Significance of bicycle taxi and handcart or wheelbarrow operations

The significance of bicycle taxi and handcart or wheelbarrow operations cannot be overemphasised. As already alluded to in chapters seven and eight, these activities are one avenue for self employment to confront the challenge of rampant unemployment. Revenues meet daily needs including food, clothes and shelter. Other uses of incomes include:

- Supporting relatives within the city and in rural areas. One respondent indicated supporting a brother to attend secondary school using income from his bicycle taxi business. Others mentioned buying fertilizer for relatives in the village.
- Saving to cater for emergencies such as sickness and bereavement and to buffer against insecurity of income. One respondent mentioned saving money to buy land on which to build a house. Others save part of their income with the hope of raising enough capital to start retail trade, possibly as market or street vendors. For example, one bicycle taxi operator reported saving money to enable his wife to open a mini-shop or hawker where they live. Another reported saving money to buy tools to establish a carpentry shop. One handcart operator used part of his savings from a hired

handcart to purchase his own, the one he was using at the time of the survey;

- Another bicycle taxi operator has constructed three houses which he is renting out at K350 per month;
- Few respondents mentioned using the money for entertainment.

This summary is enough testimony of the significance of bicycle taxis and handcarts in the livelihood strategies of the operators and their families. I found in the life story of Moses, a bicycle taxi operator, a vivid description of the significance of incomes from these operations and the diverse ways in which incomes are used. It is also a tale of the significance of social ties within the city and with family members in rural homes.

Life story of Moses

Moses is a first born son in a family of six children. He has three brothers and two sisters. He came to Mzuzu to seek employment. He was lucky enough to find a job but was dismissed after a short period of time. After losing his job he decided to join his sister who was then living in Mzuzu with her husband. His sister provided him with some money to start a business. He decided to open a grocery. At first the business grew steadily. He bought a bicycle to facilitate the running the grocery. Later on he decided to establish his own family. Economically, the situation changed when one of his younger brothers was selected for secondary school. His father back in the village could not afford to pay school fees. Moses decided to withdraw money from the business to pay the fees. This was the beginning of cash flow problems, and the grocery business did not pick up. His brother-in-law passed away. Moses had a wide range of responsibilities: pay fees for his brother and support his sister and her children financially as well as his own family. He saw an opportunity in the bicycle taxi business. With the income from the bicycle taxi business he supports his wife and their two children, one brother attending secondary, and two nieces. He is also responsible for the upkeep of his father and a sister in the village. He has two bicycles. He has plans to hire out the second to someone on contract. Besides operating a bicycle taxi, he has a *dimba* in Chiputula where he grows maize and vegetables. His aunt gave him the *dimba* (vegetable garden).

The wide range of uses of incomes from bicycle taxi and handcart operations shows how these activities are an important source of livelihood security for a large number of people, beyond those practicing these trades and visible on the streets. The invisible beneficiaries include spouses and children, and parents and siblings, just to mention a few. They are scattered over the rural-urban divide in extended families and multi-spatial households. Urban efforts to respond to needs for mobility and familial needs reinforce rural-urban interactions and serve as mechanisms for mobilizing incomes in urban settings for various activities in rural areas. Although it was difficult to quantify the magnitude of cash flows to rural areas, qualitative assessment shows that through these activities the operators are able to meet various obligations as individuals as well as members of extended families and the larger society. Drawing on studies on individual and collective agency, these activities appear to be one way by which the individual and collective values are reaffirmed. Indeed these activities are an expression of the freedom from constraints of institutional life but also, as Laguerre (1994) puts it, 'freedom as a kind of manifest destiny where the self reaffirms itself'.

Table 9.1 Leading uses of remittances

Leading uses of remittances
Daily needs and expenses (70 to 90 percent of remittances), typically labeled as consumption or as improving recipients' standard of living
Health-related expenses and education, often grouped with consumption when seen as improving standard of living
Consumer durables (stereos, televisions, washing machines)
Improvement or acquisition of housing, purchases of land or livestock
Socio-cultural investment (birth, marriage, pilgrimage, death)
Loan repayments (often loans to pay for cost of migration)
Savings
Income or employment-generating activities

Source: Sander, C. and Maimbo, S.M. (2003) *Migrant labor remittances in Africa: reducing obstacles to developmental contributions*

The significance of these activities transcends meeting the needs and obligations of individual operators; the activities have flourished partly because there are people ready to use the service being provided. These include commuters, retailers and minibus conductors among others. Bicycle taxi operators sometimes offer convenient transport to fuel stations whenever minibus operators run out of fuel on the road. The advantages of these modes of transport include speed, low cost and convenience. Bicycle taxis are faster than walking. Both bicycle taxis and handcarts are cheaper as compared to taxis and minibuses over certain distances. Both are convenient in a number of ways. They operate on roads or to locations other modes of transport do not and sometimes cannot reach. Clients are assured a door to door service and a direct route to their destinations. The operators do not delay passengers waiting for additional passengers as is common with minibus operators, and sometimes they are sent on errands. Familiarity brings trust that can hardly be cultivated or replicated by minibus operators. After talking with about ten clients, I noted that the clientele derive satisfaction from the services in a number of ways, including but not limited to:

- Speed, convenience and reliability. There are no delays for example while waiting for other passengers. A passenger to Chiputula noted that 'Even if there were minibuses I would have opted for a Sacramento. It is fast, no waiting at the depot, its quick';
- Cheap: The fare is just like that for minibuses for certain locations like Chibavi, though for some locations like Luwinga they charge a little more. The fares are also negotiable;
- Operators are trustworthy.

Most of the clients involved in the survey were male, between 15 and 40 years of age. All of them mentioned living in one of the high density traditional housing areas (THA), for example Masasa, Chibavi, Ching'ambo, Mchengautuwa, Chiputula, Zolozolo, and Sozibele. As mentioned earlier, the bicycle taxi and handcart operators reside in the same areas. These residential areas are poorly serviced by city authorities. Except for Chibavi, Zolozolo and parts of Mchengautuwa, there is no motorized public transport service to these areas. They are also well known for social ills such as prostitution and robbery. It was noted that most of the clients happened to be employed or self employed in the informal economy as shop assistants, carpenters and barbers. Considering the nature of employment and the places of residence, it can safely be argued that the bicycle taxi and handcart operators service mainly low income groups and low income residential areas. One piece of evidence is that there is no rank located to offer services to the high income residential areas like Chimaliro and Kaning'ina. In the words of one of the bicycle taxi operators, the high income residential areas are for the 'bosses' or the affluent who rarely use the bicycle taxi.

The use of bicycle taxis has spurred a growth in the number of bicycle repair shops. This is evident in the market known as Freedom Square or Hardware market and along the road to Chibavi Township. In Freedom Square there are close to 10 such repair shops while along the Chibavi road the number is much higher, which is a reflection of the volume of business along this road.

Photo 9.1 Bicycle taxis under repair in Freedom Square (Hardware) market

Conclusion

It is apparent that the bicycle taxi and handcart operators perform important social and economic roles and in a manner that cannot be replicated by the formal economy. It is encouraging that workers in the sector are proactively instituting measures to ameliorate conditions and address challenges, with or without the support of the state agents. This is a clear example of how much can be attained by grassroots players in the struggle against poverty, unemployment and underemployment. Informal economy workers comprise a disadvantaged group often perceived as incapable of effective organisation and satisfied with operating outside the regulatory framework of the state. By working with the police or other state agents, the operators gain much needed legitimacy. Yet, legitimacy does not imply acceptance as witnessed by the recent forced relocation of street vendors to designated but poorly serviced trading places. Only time will tell the future of bicycle taxi and handcart operations. Will the government proscribe bicycle and handcart taxing? Will the authorities begin to appreciate and work within real life situations or pursue idealized versions of regulation less appropriate for the informal economy of Mzuzu city? Most of the bicycle taxi operators are optimistic that the local authorities and the central government will act honourably by among other measures permitting the bicycle taxis to continue operating with minimal interference.

Chapter Ten

REFLECTIONS AND CONCLUDING DISCUSSIONS

Reflections on socio-economic informality

Large numbers of low-skilled people pour into towns and cities and look for employment opportunities to improve their economic circumstances and those of their families. Such influx creates two acute crises of unemployment and poverty on the one hand and excess pressure on or lack of the most basic facilities on the other. Most bicycle taxi and handcart or wheelbarrow operators live in high density traditional housing areas (THA) where the provision of social amenities is hardly adequate. Such informal or squatter settlements provide sanctuary to informal economy workers characterized as low income earners. Previous chapters have emphasized that as more people leave rural areas because of declining opportunities, low agricultural productivity, lack of employment opportunities and lack of access to basic physical and social infrastructure, expectations of secure employment, higher incomes and better standards of living in urban areas are rarely realized. The effect is rising levels of urban poverty.

The proliferation of informal economies in which a significant proportion of urban poor earn a living requires that analyses of work and economic life in present day cities in the developing world include the characteristics and dynamics of the informal economy. Informality is growing and is increasingly important in the process of urbanisation. At the beginning of the 1960s when most African states attained independence, this linkage was loose and largely ignored. It has since become imperative to understand what people do when the state's macro-economic policies fail. Through informality migrants avoid destitution for want of formal employment. At the same time, informality reduces the cost of providing for the needs of a growing urban population. Informality also allows the unemployed or the marginally employed to partake in a small way of resources disproportionately allocated among urban populations. From this perspective, informality is an opportunity.

Although the informal economy is not a new phenomenon, its phenomenal growth since the mid 1990s, mainly in southern Africa, is indicative of shifting economics which defy optimism for 'better' urban conditions, that is full employment, low levels of poverty and reduced inequality, on a model of formal sector growth (Meagher, 1995). In Malawi, it is likely that poverty will remain profound and widespread in both urban and rural areas (Economist Intelligence Unit, 2002: 30). High rates of rural poverty and severe inequalities in urban areas will encourage more and more people to join the informal economy. Urban poverty is not new, and nor is it the sole effect of structural adjustment policies (SAPs) of the 1980s and 1990s or indicator of economic mismanagement of the last 10 or so years as many people in Malawi are made to believe. Poverty predates the 21st century and it seems there is need for revolutionary change to overturn the situation.

That poverty – the lack of adequate means for survival – has never been solely a rural phenomenon should not be regarded as a form of solace to those charged with urban planning and development. Problems of mobility, poor housing and disparate survival strategies are real and demand adequate attention. Formal opportunities for self fulfilment simply do not abound in Malawi's towns and cities (Jimu, 2003). The rate of urbanisation and the ongoing rural-urban influx of people described at length in chapters three to five are stretching the capacity of local urban economies and by extension the national economy to provide and sustain a descent level of welfare. The informal economy, especially since the mid 1990s, is an avenue by which the poor negotiate urbanisation. The growth of informal economies indicates that there are too many people in towns and cities for limited employment opportunities, at the same time that squatter settlements proliferate due to shortage of good and affordable housing. In 1998 it was estimated that about 1.47 million urban dwellers lived below the poverty line, representing 54 percent of the urban population and 21 percent of Malawi's poor (United States Agency for International Development, 2002). Very little has changed in the area of employment creation, and there is every reason to believe that the numbers of people engaged in the informal economy will continue to grow. As Malawi enters the 21st century, some of the key factors preventing macro-economic and social development include (Dorward et al., 2003; Harrigan, 2001):

- High dependence on agriculture and lack of diversification in estate agricultural exports;
- Slow growth of smallholder agriculture exports and low productivity in the production of maize, a food crop that accounts for around 70 percent of cultivated area;

- Depressed world prices for main exports;
- Lack of other exploitable natural resources;
- Isolation and high import and export costs due to landlocked location;
- Inadequate agricultural and industrial policies to cope with rapid population and labour growth, in other words small land holdings with high population densities;
- Rising cost of energy resources;
- Economic adjustment difficulties;
- Recent collapse of the industrial economy due to exposure to outside competition;
- Poor macroeconomic management and performance with large budget deficit, high interest rates, and large devaluations of the Malawi Kwacha over the last decade;
- Poor physical infrastructure;
- Very high rates of HIV/AIDS infection with multiple debilitating effects on livelihoods and the economy.

In the midst of these challenges, the informal economy provides opportunities for negotiating economic challenges associated with rapid urbanisation and potential pathways out of poverty.

This optimism contrasts with previous scepticism of regarding the viability of the informal economy. For instance, some 30 to 40 years ago when the concept of the informal sector found a place in academic and development discourses, the common perception in official circles was that this sector was transitory and would die out when formal economies picked up (Meagher, 1995). It is now evident that this is not likely. In the case of sub Saharan Africa, accelerated export revenues of cash crops and minerals in the 1960s and 1970s stalled in the early 1980s and by the early 1990s economic and political liberalisation ushered in accelerated de-industrialisation that has swelled armies of the unemployed. Unskilled and illiterate proletarians continue to pursue a variety of activities that are not accounted for using conventional economic principles applicable in capitalist economies. They make ends meet under the most pessimistic conditions. Yet, economic policies and urban planning remain heavily biased in favour of big business ventures such as banks, factory scale industrial production and high order retail and wholesale outlets (Post, 1996). The one million Kwacha question is, how long will urban administrators and planners remain unyielding and unaccommodating to the demands of the informal economy? To date they overlook the fact that economic growth has failed to generate an expanding, efficient and modern urban sector and that, far from disappearing, informal economy activities are gaining ground, filling gaps that the formal economy is failing to bridge and in some cases levelling shortfalls created by the retreat of the formal economy as a direct result of economic liberalisation (War on Want et al., 2006) and the failure of the state to manage the economy properly. In Malawi's towns and cities informal activities are unlikely to die out even with a growth in employment opportunities in the formal or big sector.

Local authorities in Malawi's towns and cities perceive the informal economy as conflicting with appropriate aesthetic, social and economic standards (Jimu, 2005). Urbanity is considered inconsistent with the presence of informal workers in town centres (Cross, 1998: 19). As mentioned in the initial chapter, the tendency in many cases is to view urbanisation as simply an increase in the number of people living and working in towns and cities, with little or no regard for the individual and collective experiences of urbanisation. The linkage between urbanisation and the informal economy provided in this study rests upon appreciating a series of changes – economic, demographic, and political – and their associated consequences such as changes in the character and dynamics of the urban system. Everybody familiar with the past democratic and economic liberalisation experiences in Malawi will agree that the proliferation of bicycle taxi and handcart operations in Mzuzu city is a reflection of economic malaise. Dwindling employment opportunities necessitate that the urban poor engage in various informal economic activities, otherwise how would they survive when there are no welfare programmes for the unemployed? The need to survive should not disguise or overshadow the desire to advance socio-economically. The informal economy is not just a manifestation of economic crisis and the response of the poor to it but also a means through which the poor seek to express themselves and achieve some level of socio-economic independence and success (Cross, 1998). Because the informal economy has become much more pronounced in the last 12 to 15 years, and in the case of bicycle taxis in Mzuzu city over the last two to three years, I would agree with Englund (2002) that the enhanced liberalisation of the economy in the 1990s opened opportunities for entrepreneurial spirit that go beyond spatial limits.

Bicycle taxi and handcart or wheelbarrow operators demonstrate how the urban poor earn a living, negotiate urbanisation and also contribute to the construction of urban socio-economic landscapes. Several points are worth repeating in this regard.

First, bicycle taxis and handcarts contribute significantly to livelihoods. Despite the gaps of information pertaining to incomes earned by bicycle taxi and handcart operators, it appears that daily incomes are higher and more regular than in other informal occupations. On average, daily incomes range from an equivalent of US$2 to US$7 per day. At face value the operators live above the poverty line, but when the number of dependents is factored in, per capita income falls to less than US$1 per day. The operators are by no means the poorest of the poor. Incomes are comparable to incomes in Uganda where bicycle taxi operators were reported to earn about 5000 Shillings a day (equivalent to US$3.00 per day) (BBC, 2001) and in Burundi where it was estimated that bicycle taxi operators earned between 2000 and 3000 Burundi Francs a day, an equivalent of R12 (12 Rand) (IOL South Africa, 2005), which in Malawi Kwacha (at the rate of 1 Rand = MWK 22.00) is equal to K260.00 or about US$1.86 per day. In nominal terms, the Malawian bicycle taxi operators earn much more than their counterparts in Uganda and Burundi. However, the situation could be different if inflation and the purchasing power of the various currencies were taken into account.

Experiences of bicycle taxi operators Burundi

Bicycle taxi operators in East Africa experience numerous challenges, for example in Burundi and Uganda. In Burundi the bicycle taxi operators were in 2002 caught up in the civil war and the government seized hundreds of bicycle taxis in Bujumbura on suspicion that their operators were supporting the rebels by transporting combatants. The ethnic divide played a part in the misunderstanding and misrepresentation in the sense that most of the bicycle taxi operators were of Hutu ethnicity at a time when the Hutu militias were fighting a Tutsi dominated government and army. The seizure of bicycles was unjustified and deprived the operators from make a living. The government justified the anti-poor actions by claiming that the move would reduce a rising number of traffic accidents blamed on the bicycle taxis. The decision to ban bicycle taxis was unpopular and unenforceable, and it meant putting people out of work and denying thousands a livelihood (IOL South Africa, 2005).

Second, from a social development point of view, because most of the operators are self employed, it can be argued that this form of business allows the marginally employed to earn a relatively descent income as compared to theft, prostitution, and destitution. Also worth repeating is that these operators meet transport needs of both formal and informal workers.

Third, it is obvious from the demographic characteristics presented in chapter seven that these activities are dominated by young men in their 20s and 30s. Most of them are married and they work to support their families. Considering the traditional extended family system prevailing in Malawi, income earned through these informal activities constitutes an important part of the income and livelihood strategy of a lot of people spread in both urban and rural areas. In multi-spatial household units, such incomes are seen as a mechanism by which livelihood security and success is secured by a stay in town. This survey provides ample evidence of cash flows from cities to rural homes, yet most operators are unsure about the long term fulfilment of their aspirations. Englund (2002: 150) observed similar sentiments among migrants living in Chinsapo, Lilongwe. He observed that '[m]any plan to intensify cultivation in their village of origin through the profits they have made in town, or open a grocery or some other small-scale enterprise there'. For such individuals 'moving between town and country often becomes a way of life, with important social ties being established in both settings'. Life stories of bicycle taxi and handcart or wheelbarrow operators collected in this study provide evidence of multi-spatial households as noted in the study by Englund in Chinsapo.

Fourth, from the demographic characteristics of the operators, it is also evident that the bicycle taxi and handcart operators are in the low income category. All the operators live in high density traditional housing areas. They rent and live in grass thatched or iron sheet roofed houses in residential areas associated with lack of essential amenities such as water, public transport and electricity. Therefore, bicycle taxi and handcart or wheelbarrow operations represent business opportunities for the poor, serving mostly underprivileged segments of society. In this regard, the bicycle taxi and handcart or wheelbarrow operations make a remarkable contribution towards the livelihoods of people in the slums. They also transform urban realities by linking various activities and spaces in ways unknown before.

Fifth, though not appreciated by authorities, bicycle taxis and handcarts stand out as environmentally friendly modes of transport. They are essentially non-polluting and do not need big roads and lots of parking space (BBC, 2001). As parking problems become acute it may become a policy option to encourage the use of bicycles and bicycle taxis in the central business districts or city centres of the towns and cities of Malawi. If this can be done now, it may help avoid the problems of air pollution endemic in the populous cities of Asia and other parts of the developed world.

The informal economy is sometimes portrayed as a social problem. In the case of bicycle taxi and handcart operators, they are sometimes portrayed as such in relation to road accidents and overcrowding that comes when operators, especially handcart operators, block roads with the heavy and oversized loads they are often required to move. In this respect, it is important to understand that the term 'social problem' is controversial. Rubington and Weinberg (1977) defined a social problem as an alleged situation that is incompatible with the values (economic, social, cultural, political and environmental) of a significant number of people, who agree that action is needed. As stated in the introductory chapter, a phenomenon becomes a problem once it is designated as harmful and calls are made for improvement. Sociologists and political scientists agree that, in general, people who are most successful in defining social problems are those who are more organized, in positions of leadership and more powerful in economic, social and political affairs (Outhwaite and Bottomore, 1993). Such people have no use for the services offered by bicycle taxi and handcart operators.

As noted in the lists in chapter six of challenges of bicycle taxi and handcart operators and how to overcome them, government agents have a role to play in improving conditions for the operators and other informal economy workers. Efforts to relocate informal workers from the streets to designated markets with or without necessary amenities and with little regard to impacts on livelihoods have fuelled pessimism regarding the capacity and willingness of the government to support the informal economy. However, earlier steps taken by the government to provide loans to small scale businesses remain a talking point and has in many quarters aroused and sustained a sense of optimism. The government can do a better job of improving roads in the city. The traffic police can play a catalytic role by intensifying checks on compliance with the requirement that all bicycle taxi operators have identity cards and use roadworthy bicycles. Another need is training programs on traffic rules for pedestrians, cyclists as well as motorists to prevent accidents. In summary, the issues that emerged during interviews and focus group discussions centred on facilitating the free flow of traffic and safety on the roads as well as addressing financial challenges that limit the growth of meaningful informal enterprises. The issues discussed include:

- Extension of credit facilities to the operators so they may set up small enterprises producing tradable goods or expand existing ones. The Malawi Rural Development Fund (MARDEF) loan facility could be one of the schemes to make a difference in the lives of bicycle taxi and handcart operators and seems appropriate because a large percentage of the operators have plans to quit and establish other meaningful businesses;
- Creation of more viable and meaningful employment opportunities. The operators are of the view that the government should provide an enabling investment environment for local and foreign companies so that jobs become available to as many young people as possible;
- Informal education classes on complementary skills such as enterprise management, marketing and transfer of new technologies;
- Improvement in security. The issue of security is high on the government's development agenda as announced by the

state president on numerous occasions. Improved security will facilitate bicycle taxi operators more than handcart operators because all the reported cases of robbery and theft involved bicycles operators. Improved road security will help all road users;

- As for the problem of instability of incomes, individual operators and the associations ought to promote and regulate the bicycle taxi and handcart operations through equitable and cordial rationing of clients, and hence incomes;
- Authorities should begin to intervene in the working life of people employed as shop assistants to address issues of wages and other working conditions;
- The self-employed in the informal economy need also to begin thinking seriously about forming organisations that regulate the business as well as act as a mouthpiece with the traffic authorities and with the local government.

Further, considering the socio-economic value of the activities in question it is evident, though by no means self explanatory to people unfamiliar with the manner and conduct of business in the informal economy, that the bicycle taxi and handcart operators play a vital role in the construction of the socio-economic landscapes and identities of Mzuzu city. Addressing challenges mentioned in chapter six and acting on recommendations in this last chapter will go a long way towards improving business in the two sub-sectors, as well as alleviating bottlenecks experienced by informal economy workers in general. Such measures may also improve the efficaciousness of urban life, and the informal economy would no longer appear a menace, nuisance or inconvenience to proper urban development, mobility and social interaction.

Future directions

This study provides new information about emerging and imaginative informal economy activities, other than trading, undertaken in Mzuzu and several rural towns in Malawi. At the moment, nobody knows how many bicycle taxi and handcart operators are working in Mzuzu and the country as a whole. This reflects in part the absence of a regulatory framework and also disinterest of authorities. The informal economy is characterized as a less productive sector and quite often dismissed altogether, with the assumption that informal workers make very little contribution to the economy. However, as this study has shown, the operators play a vital role in economic processes of Mzuzu city. The situation must be similar in other centres where bicycle taxis operate. The opportunities and challenges experienced by bicycle taxi and wheelbarrow operators provide justification for policy intervention to safeguard seemingly marginal livelihood strategies. The study should be seen as a wake up call to authorities and the public at large to begin to appreciate grassroots ingenuity in the midst of disparaging and debilitating economic situations.

This study has not exhausted all the issues we must understand in coming to grips with the informal economy of Malawi in general and bicycle taxi and handcart or wheelbarrow operators in particular. For instance, there is need to investigate the organisational dynamics of bicycle taxi and handcart or wheelbarrow operators. Very little is known about this although this study attempted to scout for some information. The gaps are numerous and there is more to be learnt to correct inconsistencies in the data. Since the relocation of street vendors in Mzuzu in the first half of 2006, informal businesses there experienced a downturn. As business is now picking up, it is necessary to investigate the impact of the restructuring of the informal economy in general and on bicycle taxi and handcart operations in particular. Other issues that might merit further investigation are multi-tasking and engagement in multiple livelihood activities, informal economy challenges outlined in chapter six, and effectiveness of the coping strategies mentioned by the operators, as well as government involvement in promoting informal livelihood strategies and informal non-motorized transport. Considering that entry and exits in informal businesses tend to be on the high side, as evidenced by the desire to exit reported in this study, it may also be enlightening to investigate exits and entries and their impacts on other economic activities, particularly in the informal sector. Another dimension has to do with the social conditions of informal economy workers as well as how they project their stay in towns and cities. This hinges on understanding urban planning and the political context. Understanding the dynamics of the connection between informality and urbanisation in Malawi requires that all these issues be investigated, in one big study or a number of separate studies. Such research should inform policy formulation, involve informal economy workers, and contribute to improved livelihood opportunities and living conditions of low income people engaged in the informal economy while also seeking to improve housing, infrastructure, and the physical environmental.

Bibliography

AFRODAD (African Forum and Network on Debt and Development) (2005) *The politics of the MGDs and Malawi: a critical appraisal of the global partnership for development (Goal 8).* www.afrodad.org/downloads/publications/MDGs%20Malawi.pdf (last accessed on 12 August 2008)

Ajayi, O.O. (1996) Problems of surveying the informal sector: the case of Nigeria. In Herman, B. and Stoffers, W. (eds.), *Unveiling the informal sector: more than counting heads.* Aldershot, United Kingdom: Avebury.

Altman, M. (2007) *What are the policy implications of the informal sector becoming the informal economy?* Concept paper prepared for IZA/World Bank conference on employment and development, Bonn, Germany, June 8-9.

BBC News (2001) *Bicycle taxi wars in eastern Uganda.* 6 March, 16:51 GMT.

Benson, T. (2002) *Malawi: an atlas of social statistics.* Zomba, Malawi: National Statistical Office; Washington, DC, USA: International Food Policy Research Institute.

Bernabè, S. (2002) *Informal employment in countries in transition: a conceptual framework.* Case paper 56, Centre for Analysis of Social Exclusion, London School of Economics, United Kingdom.

Blantyre City Assembly (2000) *Urban Structure Plan.* Volumes I and III.

Blantyre Newspapers Limited (1985a) 'Mzuzu is now a city', *Malawi News*, September 7-13, 1985.

Blantyre Newspapers Limited (1985b) 'Mzuzu wins new status', *Malawi News*, September 28 - October 4, 1985.

Brinkhoff, T. (2003) Tables of towns of Malawi. www.citypopulation.de/Malawi.html (last accessed on 12 August 2008)

Briscoe, A. (1995) *The promotion of small and micro-enterprises in southern Africa.* Southern Africa Development Community (SADC).

Bromley, R. (1978) The urban informal sector: why is it worth discussing. In Bromley, R. (ed.) *The urban informal sector: critical perspectives on employment and housing policies,* Swansea, United Kingdom: Pergamon.

Bromley, R. (1997) Working in the streets of Cali, Columbia: survival strategy, necessity, or unavoidable evil? In Gugler, J. (ed.), *Cities in the developing world: issues, theory and policy*. Oxford, United Kingdom: Oxford University Press.

Bromley, R.D.F. (1998) Informal commerce: expansion and exclusion in the historical center of the Latin American City. *International Journal of Urban and Regional Research*, 22(2), pp. 245-264.

Brown, A. (2006) Challenging street livelihoods. In Brown, A. (ed.), *Contested space: street trading, public space, and livelihoods in developing cities*. Rugby, Warwickshire, United Kingdom: Intermediate Technology.

Brown, A. and Lloyd-Jones, T. (2002) Spatial planning, access and infrastructure. In Rakodi, C. and Lloyd-Jones, T. (eds.), *Urban livelihoods: a people-centred approach to reducing poverty*, pp. 188-204. London, United Kingdom: Earthscan.

Bryceson, D. (1996) De-agrarianization and rural employment generation in sub Saharan Africa: a sectoral perspective. *World Development*, 24(1), pp. 97-111.

Button, K. and Ndoh, N. (1991) *Vehicle ownership and use forecasting in low income countries*. Crowthorne, United Kingdom: Transport and Road Research Laboratory.

Campbell, R. (2000) Malawi. In *African Review*, 23rd edition, pp. 171-176. London, United Kingdom: Walden.

Chambers, R. (1989) Vulnerability, coping and policy. *Institute of Development Studies Bulletin*, 20(2), pp. 1-7.

Chipeta, M. (1990) Status of the informal sector in Malawi. *Southern Africa*, 3(11), SAPES.

Chirwa, J. (2000) *A reconnaissance study of social, economic and environmental impact of street vending in Malawi: a case study of Mzuzu city*. Unpublished Geography Thesis, University of Malawi.

Colleye, P.O. (1996) Mali. In Webster, L. and Fidler, P. (eds.), *The informal sector and microfinance institutions in West Africa*. Washington, DC, USA: The World Bank.

Cross, J.C. (1998) *Informal politics: street vendors and the state in Mexico*. Stanford, California, USA: Stanford University Press.

Dasgupta, B. (1973) Calcutta's informal sector. *IDS Bulletin*, 5(2/3), University of Sussex, pp. 53-75.

Devereux, S. (2002) 'State of Disaster: Causes, Consequences & Policy Lessons from Malawi' An ActionAID Report on food crisis in Malawi Commissioned by ActionAid Malawi

Dorward, A., Morrison, J., Poulton, C. and Tchale, H. (2003) *Disaggregated impacts of agricultural policy reform on rural households in Malawi.* Paper presented at the first meeting of the OECD Global Forum on Agriculture: Designing and Implementing pro-Poor Agricultural Policies, Paris, December, 10-11, 2003.

Douglas, J. (2000) Malawi: Blantyre and Lilongwe. *Travel Africa Edition Thirteen.* www.travelafricamag.com/index2.php?option=com_content&do_pdf=1&id=345 (last accessed on 12 August 2007)

Economic Policy Institute/Global Policy Network (undated) 'The Informal Economy' www.epi.org/newsroom/releases/2005/03/050301GPN_Informal_Fact_Sheet.pdf (last accessed on 27 August 2008)

Economist Intelligence Unit (EIU) (1986-1994) *Malawi: country profile.*

Economist Intelligence Unit (1995-6) *Malawi: country profile.*

Economist Intelligence Unit (1997-8) *Malawi: country profile.*

Economist Intelligence Unit (2000) *Malawi: country profile.*

Economist Intelligence Unit (2001) *Malawi: country profile.*

Economist Intelligence Unit (2002) *Malawi: country profile.*

Ellis, F. and Freeman, A. (2002) *Rural livelihoods and poverty reduction strategies in four African countries.* LADDER working paper no. 30. Overseas Development Group (ODG), University of East Anglia, Norwich, United Kingdom; ICRISAT, Nairobi, Kenya.

Ellis, F., Kutengule, M. and Nyasulu, A. (2003) Livelihood and rural poverty reduction in Malawi. *World Development,* 31(9), p. 1495-1510.

Emizet, K.N.L.F. (1998) Confronting leaders at the apex of the state: the growth of the unofficial economy in Congo. *African Studies Review,* 41(1), pp. 99-137.

Englund, H. (2000) The dead hand of human rights: contrasting Christianities in post-transition Malawi. *The Journal of Modern African Studies,* 38(4), pp. 579-603.

Englund, H. (2002) The village in the city, the city in the village: migrants in Lilongwe. *Journal of Southern African Studies,* 28(1), pp 37-154.

Esim, S. (1996) Guinea Bissau. In Webster, L. and Fidler, P. (eds.), *The informal sector and microfinance institutions in West Africa,* pp. 139-152. Washington, DC, USA: World Bank.

Fapohunda, O.J. (1985) *The informal sector of Lagos: an inquiry into urban employment.* Lagos, Nigeria: University Press.

Fidler, P. and Webster, L. (1996) The informal sector of West Africa. In Webster, L. and Fidler, P. (eds.) *The informal sector and microfinance institutions in West Africa,* pp. 5-20. Washington, DC, USA: International Bank for Reconstruction and Development/World Bank.

Friedman, M. and Hambridge, M. (1991) The informal sector and gender and development. In Preston-Whyte, E. and Rogerson, C. (eds.), *South Africa's informal sector.* Cape Town, South Africa: Oxford University Press.

Goldthorpe, J.E. (1996) *The sociology of post-colonial societies: economic disparity, cultural diversity and development.* New York, New York, USA: Cambridge University Press.

Green, C. and Baden, S. (1994) *Women and development in Malawi.* Report prepared for the Commission of European Communities Directorate-General for Development, Institute of Development Studies, University of Sussex, Brighton, United Kingdom.

Harrigan, J. (2001) *From dictatorship to democracy: economic policy in Malawi 1964-2000.* Aldershot, United Kingdom: Ashgate.

Hart, K. (1973) Informal income opportunities and urban employment in Ghana. *Journal of Modern African Studies,* 11(1), pp. 61-89.

Hart, K. (2006) *Informal economy.* www.thememorybank.co.uk/2006/12/18/informal-economy/#more-106 (last accessed on 17 August 2008)

Hart, K. (2007) *The urban informal economy in retrospect.* www.thememorybank.co.uk/2007/06/08/the-urban-informal-eocnomy-in-retrospect (last accessed on 17 August 2008)

Hope, K.R. Sr. (1996) *Development in the third world: from policy failure to policy reform.* Armonk, New York, USA: Sharpe.

Hope, K.R. Sr. (1997) *African political economy: contemporary issues in development,* Armonk, New York, USA: Sharpe.

Hope, K.R. Sr. (2001) Indigenous small enterprise development in Africa: growth and impact of the subterranean economy. *European Journal of Development Research,* 13(1), pp. 30-46.

Hornby, W.F. and Jones, M. (1991) *An introduction to settlement geography.* Cambridge, United Kingdom: Cambridge University Press.

Humphrey, D. (1974) *Malawi since 1964: economic development, progress and prospects.* Zomba, Malawi: Department of Economics, University of Malawi.

Hussmanns, R. (1996) ILO's recommendations on methodologies concerning informal sector data collection. In Herman, B. and Stoffers, W. (eds.) *Unveiling the informal sector: more than counting heads*, pp. 15-29. Aldershot, United Kingdom: Avebury.

Ilife, J. (1987) *The African poor: a history*. New York, New York, USA: Cambridge University Press.

IOL South Africa (2005) 'Burundi President suspends bicycle taxi ban' 25 April 2005 www.zerocouriers.com/?p=7 or www.iol.co.za/index.php?set_id=1&click_id=68&art_id=q w1114524902539B653 (last accessed on 27 August 2008)

IRIN (2004) Malawi: rapid urbanization places burden on already strained resources. Johannesburg, 7 Jul 2004 (IRIN) www.irinnews.org/report.asp?ReportID=42058&SelectRegi on=Southern_Africa&SelectCountry=MALAWI (last accessed on 19 January 2006)

Jimu, I.M. (2003) *Appropriation and mediation of urban spaces: growth, dynamics and politics of street vending in Blantyre, Malawi.* Unpublished MA Thesis, School of Graduate Studies (Department of Sociology), University of Botswana.

Jimu, I.M. (2005) Negotiated economic opportunity and power: perceptions and perspectives of street vending in Malawi. *Africa Development*, 30(4), pp. 35-51.

Kalipeni, E. (1993) *Contained urban growth in post independence Malawi*. Paper presented at the African Association of Political Science (AAPS) 20th anniversary bi-annual congress on 'Africa in the post Cold War period: governing African cities' held in Dar es Salaam, Tanzania, 18-21 January.

Kaul, C. and Tomaselli-Moschovitis, V.C. (eds.) (1999) *Statistical handbook on poverty in the developing world*. Phoenix, Arizona, USA: Oryx.

Kawonga, A.J.C. (2006) *An overview of mobility in Malawi* www.bremen-initiative.de/lib/papers/malawi.pdf (accessed November 2006)

Knox, P.L. (1994) *Urbanization: an introduction to urban geography*. Englewood Cliffs, New Jersey, USA: Prentice Hall.

Laguerre, M.S. (1994) *The informal city*, London, United Kingdom: MacMillan.

Lipton, M. (1977) *Why poor people stay poor: a study of urban bias in World Development*, London, United Kingdom: Temple Smith.

Lourenco-Lindell, I. (2002) *Walking the tight rope: informal livelihoods and social networks in a West African city*. Edsbruk, Sweden: Akademitryck AB.

MacPherson, S. and Silburn, R. (1998) The meaning and measurement of poverty. In Dixon, J. and Macarov, D. (eds.), *Poverty: a persistent global reality*. London, United Kingdom: Routledge.

Meagher, K. (1995) Crisis, informalization and the urban informal sector in sub-Saharan Africa. *Development and Change*, 26(2), pp. 259-284.

Minde, I.J. and Nakhumwa, T.O. (1998) Unrecorded cross-border trade between Malawi and neighbouring countries. Technical paper no. 90. Productive Sector Growth and Environment Office of Sustainable Development Bureau for Africa, USAID.

Mitullah, W. (2003) Street vending in African cities: a synthesis of empirical findings for Kenya, Cote d'Ivoire, Ghana, Zimbabwe, Uganda and South Africa. Background paper for the 2005 World Development Report, Institute for Development Studies, University of Nairobi, www.wiego.org/papers/2005/unifem/24_Mitullah_Streetv ending_African_Cities.pdf (last accessed on 19 August 2008)

Moser, C. (1978) Informal sector or petty production: dualism or dependence in urban development. *World Development*, 6(9/10), pp. 1041-1064.

Murry, A.J. (1991) *No money, no honey: a study of street traders and prostitutes in Jakarta*. Singapore City, Singapore: Oxford University Press.

Mwase, G.S. (1970) *Strike a blow and die: a classic story of the Chilembwe Rising*. London, United Kingdom: Heineman.

National Statistical Office (2002) *Malawi population and housing census*. Analytical report, 1998 census.

Nattrass, N.J. (1987) Street trading in Transkei: a struggle against poverty, persecution and prosecution. *World Development*, 15(7), pp. 861-875.

Niger-Thomas, M. (2000) *'Buying futures': the upsurge of female entrepreneurs crossing the formal/informal divide in south Cameroon*. PhD Thesis, University of Leiden, Netherlands.

Nyamnjoh, F.B. (2002) 'A child is one person's only in the womb': domestication, agency and subjectivity in the Cameroonian grassfields. In Werbner, R. (ed.) *Postcolonial subjectivities in Africa*, pp. 111-138. London, United Kingdom: Zed.

O'Connor, A. (1991) *Poverty in Africa: a geographical approach.* London, United Kingdom: Belhaven.

Orr, A. and Makawa, J. (2000) *Micro-entrepreneurship in Malawi.* Lilongwe, Malawi: National Economic Council.

Orr, A., Mwale, D. and Saiti, D. (2001) Market liberalization, household food security and the rural poor in Malawi. *European Journal of Development Research*, 13(1), pp. 147-69.

Orr, A. and Orr, S. (2002) *Agriculture and micro enterprise in Malawi's rural South.* Agricultural Research and Extension Network (AgREN) paper no. 119. Overseas Development Institute (ODI), London, United Kingdom. www.odi.org.uk/networks/agren/papers/agrenpaper_119.pdf (last accessed 19 August 2008)

Outhwaite, W. and Bottomore, T. (1993) *The Blackwell dictionary of twentieth-century social thought.* Oxford, United Kingdom: Blackwell.

Peterson, W. (1965) *Urban policies in Africa and Asia.* Presented at the conference on international and comparative urban studies in American higher education, Rutgers, The State University, New Brunswick, New Jersey, USA, 8 June.

Phiri, F. (2004) *Malawi: AIDS worsens the woes of urbanization.* www.nyu.edu/globalbeat/GIN072604.html (last accessed on 19 January 2006)

Francis Tayanjah-Phiri, F.T. 'Mzuzu: On the fast lane', *The Nation,* October 17, 2005

Post, J. (1996) *Space for small enterprises: reflections on urban livelihood and planning in the Sudan.* Amsterdam, Netherlands: Thesis Publishers.

Pryor, F.C. (1990) *The political economy of poverty, equity and growth: Malawi and Madagascar.* Oxford, United Kingdom: Oxford University Press.

Republic of Malawi (1977 &1998) *Population census: preliminary reports.*

Republic of Malawi (1987) *National physical development plan*, Vol. 1. Policy document, Department of town and country planning, Office of the President and Cabinet (OPC).

Republic of Malawi (1994) *Economic report.* Zomba, Malawi: Government Printer.

Republic of Malawi (1995) Policy framework for poverty alleviation programme. Lilongwe, Malawi: Poverty alleviation programme coordinating unit, Ministry of Economic Planning and Development.

Republic of Malawi (1998) *Population and housing census*. Zomba, Malawi: National Statistical Office.

Republic of Malawi (2000a) *The state of Malawi's poor: who they are*. Poverty Monitoring Systems (PMS) briefing no. 3. Zomba, Malawi: National Statistical Office.

Republic of Malawi (2000b) *GEMINI Micro and Small Enterprise (MSE) baseline survey*. Zomba, Malawi: National Statistical Office.

Republic of Malawi (2000c) *The state of Malawi's poor: their economic characteristics*. Poverty Monitoring Systems (PMS) briefing no. 6. Zomba, Malawi: National Statistical Office.

Republic of Malawi (2000d) *The state of Malawi's poor: the incidence, depth, and severity of poverty*. Poverty Monitoring Systems (PMS) briefing no. 2 (revised). Zomba, Malawi: National Statistical Office.

Republic of Malawi (2002) *Malawi Poverty Reduction Strategy Paper (MPRSP)*. Lilongwe, Malawi.

Republic of Malawi (2003) *Malawi in figures 2000*. Zomba, Malawi: National Statistical Office.

Rodrigue, J.P (2008) 'Urban Transport Problems' http://people.hofstra.edu/geotrans/eng/ch6en/conc6en/ch6c4en.html (accessed 26/02/08)

Rotberg, R.T. (ed.) (1970) *Strike a blow and die: a classic story of the Chilembwe Rising*. London, United Kingdom: Heineman.

Rogerson, C.M. and Beavon, K.S.O. (1985) A tradition of repression: the street traders of Johannesburg. In Bromley, R. (ed.), *Planning for small enterprises in third world cities*, pp. 233-245. Oxford, United Kingdom: Pergamon.

Rogerson, C.M. and Hart, D.M. (1989) The struggle for the streets: deregulation and hawking in South Africa's major urban areas. *Social Dynamics*, Centre for African Studies, University of Cape Town, South Africa, Vol. 15(1), pp. 29-45.

Rondinelli, D.A. (1988) *Market towns and urban-rural linkages*. Paper presented at the USAID sponsored conference on agricultural growth and market town development, Lilongwe, Malawi.

Rubington, E. and Weinberg, M.S. (1977) *The study of social problems: five perspectives*. New York, New York, USA: Oxford University Press.

Sander, C. and Maimbo, S.M. (2003) Migrant labour remittances in Africa: reducing obstacles to developmental contributions. Africa region working paper no. 64.

www.worldbank.org/afr/wps/index.htm (last accessed on 19 August 2008)

Santos, M. (1979) *The shared space: the two circuits of the urban economy in underdeveloped countries.* London, United Kingdom: Methuen.

Satterthwaite, D. (2000) *Seeking an understanding of poverty that recognizes rural-urban differences and rural-urban linkages.* Paper presented at the World Bank's urban forum on urban poverty reduction in the 21st century, April. International Institute for Environment and Development (IIED).

Scott, A.J. (1980) *The urban land nexus and the State,* London, United Kingdom: Pion.

Sinclair, S.W. (1978) *Urbanisation and labour markets in developing countries.* London, United Kingdom: Croom Helm.

Singini, E.E. (undated) *People of Mzuzu: late 1800s to mid 1990s.* Lilongwe, Malawi: Likuni Press and Publishing House.

de Soto, H. (1989) *The other path: the invisible revolution in the third world,* translated by J. Abbot. New York, New York, USA: Harper and Row.

Stambuli, P.K (2002) *Political change, economic transition and catalysis of IMF/World Bank economic models: the case of Malawi.* Paper presented at a conference on 'Malawi after Banda: perspectives in a regional African context,' Centre of Commonwealth Studies, University of Stirling, Scotland.

Tacoli, C. (1998) *Bridging the divide: rural-urban interactions and livelihood strategies.* Gatekeeper series no. SA77. International Institute for Environment and Development (IIED).

Tellegen, N. (1997) *Rural enterprises in Malawi: necessity or opportunity?* Aldershot, Hampshire, United Kingdom: Ashgate.

Thomas, A. (2000) Poverty and the 'end of development'. In Allen, T. and Thomas, A. (eds.) *Poverty and development into the 21st century.* Oxford, United Kingdom: The Open University in Association with Oxford University Press.

Tokman, V. (1978) An exploration into the nature of informal-formal sector relationships. *World Development,* 6(9/10), pp. 1065-75.

Torres, L. (2000) *The smoking business: tobacco workers in Malawi.* FAFO Institute for Applied Social Science.

United Nations (1996) *Informal sector development in Africa.* New York, New York, USA: United Nations.

United Nations (2003) *World urbanization prospects: the 2003 revision population database.* http://esa.un.org/unup (last accessed on 19 January 2006)

United Nations (2004) *Malawi is fastest urbanizing country in the world* www.scoop.co.nz/stories/WO0407/S00083.htm (last accessed on 18 August 2008)

United Nations (2007) *World urbanization prospects: the 2007 revision population database.* http://esa.un.org/unup (last accessed on 18 August 2008)

United States Agency for International Development (2002) *Making cities work.* Malawi.

Valdivia, C. and Quiroz, R. (2001) *Rural livelihood strategies, assets and economic portfolios in coping with climatic perturbations: a case study of the Bolivian Andes.* Paper presented at the social organization and land management session of the workshop on integrated natural resource management for sustainable agriculture, forestry and fisheries of the International Center for Tropical Agriculture, 28-31 August, CIAT, Cali, Colombia.

Walker, A. (1996) Guinea. In Webster, L. and Fidler, P. (eds.), *The informal sector and microfinance institutions in West Africa,* pp. 127-138. Washington DC: World Bank.

War on Want (WOW), Workers Education Association of Zambia (WEAZ) and Alliance for Zambian Informal Economy Associations (AZIEA) (2006) *Forces for change: informal economy organisations in Africa.* London, United Kingdom: War on Want.

Whiteside, M. (1998) *When the whole is more than the sum of the parts: the effects of cross-border interactions on livelihood security in southern Malawi and northern Mozambique.* A report for Oxfam Great Britain.

Wobst, P., Lofgren, H., Tchale, H., and Morrison J. (2004) *Pro-poor development strategies for Malawi: an economy-wide analysis of alternative policy scenarios.* Institutions and economic policies for pro-poor agricultural growth, DFID, United Kingdom (R7989).

World Bank (1980, 1985, 1990, 1997, 2000) *World Development Report.* New York, New York, USA: Oxford University Press.

www.ingramcontent.com/pod-product-compliance
Lightning Source LLC
Chambersburg PA
CBHW021820270326
41932CB00007B/264